Seven Days In Dublin
The Ultimate Short Stay Guide

SHANE KENNEDY

Gill & Macmillan

Gill & Macmillan Ltd
Hume Avenue
Park West
Dublin 12

with associated companies throughout the world
www.gillmacmillan.ie

© 2001 Shane Kennedy
0 7171 3078 9

Typeset in Sabon Roman 10.5pt by Andy Gilsenan, Dublin
Printed by The Guernsey Press, Guernsey
Illustrations by Michael Fewer
Maps on pages 110, 128, 142 and 143 by Design Image

*The paper used in this book is made from the wood pulp of managed
forests. For every tree felled, at least one tree is planted, thereby
renewing natural resources.*

5 4 3 2 1

Contents

INTRODUCTION   VII
A History of the City in 347 words   vii
Get Oriented   viii
One-day Special   ix

SEVEN DAYS IN DUBLIN: GETTING YOUR BEARINGS   XI
Arrival at the Airport   xi
Arrival at the Ferryport   xii
Arrival at Dun Laoghaire   xiii
Arrival by Rail   xiii
Essential Information   xiii
Some of the Best   xvi
Ten Essential Pubs   xix
Pubs without Television and Musak   xxii
Ten Restaurants   xxiv
Some Things You Can't Do Anywhere Else xxvii
Gay and Lesbian Dublin   xxix
Nightlife   xxxi
Top Ten Rainy Day Options   xxxi

DAY 1 TRINITY AND THE GEORGIAN CITY   1
Trinity   1
College Green   10
Grafton Street   13
St Stephen's Green   16
The Georgian Squares   27

DAY 2 TEMPLE BAR AND THE OLD CITY 39
    Temple Bar 39
    Civic Offices 44
    Christ Church 46
    St Patrick's Cathedral 48
    Marsh's Library 50
    Dublin Castle 56
    City Hall 58

DAY 3 THE QUAYS AND THE PARK 62
    Heuston Station 65
    Royal Hospital/IMMA 66
    Kilmainham Jail 67
    National Museum at Collins' Barracks 74
    Smithfield 76
    St Michan's 78
    Four Courts 78
    The Custom House 81
    IFSC 85

DAY 4 NORTH INNER CITY 87
    O'Connell Street 88
    Rotunda 94
    Parnell Square 95
    Hugh Lane Gallery 96
    Dublin Writers' Museum 97
    Around Mountjoy Square 101
    Gate Theatre 102
    The Pro-Cathedral 105
    Abbey Theatre 106

DAY 5 AROUND THE SUBURBS 111
    RDS 111
    Drimnagh Castle 113
    Rathfarnham Castle 113
    Rathmines and Rathgar 114

Mount Jerome Cemetery 117
The National Botanic Gardens 120
Prospect (Glasnevin) Cemetery 120
Casino 122
Bull Island 124
Malahide and Malahide Castle 125

DAY 6 DART AROUND THE COAST 129
Howth 130
Sutton 134
Clontarf 134
Booterstown and Blackrock 136
Dun Laoghaire 136
Dalkey 140
Bray 141
Greystones 141

DAY 7 OUT OF TOWN 144
County Wicklow 144
Enniskerry 147
Powerscourt 147
County Meath 160
Boyne Valley 163

INDEX 170

The publishers are grateful to the Ordnance Survey Office
for permission to reproduce sections of the street maps of
Dublin on pages xxxii, 38, 60, 61 and 86.

Introduction

A History of the City in 347 words

Dublin started as a Viking trading settlement in the middle of the tenth century. Location was the key to its quick ascendancy among Irish towns. It commanded the shortest crossing to a major port in Britain. By the time the Normans arrived in Ireland in the late twelfth century, this was crucial: Dublin maintained the best communications between the English crown and its new lordship in Ireland.

The city first developed on the rising ground south of the river where Christ Church now is. The English established their principal citadel in this area, although Dublin Castle was later described by one disgruntled governor as 'the worst castle in the worst site in Christendom'. Throughout the medieval and early modern periods, the city's importance was entirely ecclesiastical and strategic. It was not a centre of learning, or fashion or commerce.

The foundation of Trinity College in 1592 was a landmark event but the city did not really develop until the long peace of the eighteenth century. Then the series of fine, wide Georgian streets and noble public buildings that are Dublin's greatest boast were built. A semi-autonomous parliament of the Anglo-Irish colonial élite provided a focus for social life and the city flourished.

This parliament dissolved itself in 1800 under the terms of

the Act of Union and Ireland became a full part of the metropolitan British state, a situation not reversed until Irish independence in 1922 (Northern Ireland always excepted). The union years saw Dublin decline. Fine old houses were gradually abandoned by the aristocracy and became hideous tenement warrens. The city missed out on the Industrial Revolution. By the time Joyce immortalised it, it had become 'the centre of paralysis' in his famous phrase.

Independence restored some of its natural function but there was still much poverty and shabbiness. The 1960s boom proved to be a false dawn. Only in the 1990s has there been real evidence of a city reinventing and revitalising itself. There is still much to be done: alongside the splendour, there are many areas of dereliction and neglect. Long live the boom!

Get Orientated

If you are a short-term tourist in Dublin, here is the essential fix on the city. It is divided by the River Liffey, which flows west to east into Dublin Bay. The south side is richer and more fashionable than the north side. Most — but by no means all — of what you have come to see lies south of the river. The northside-southside rivalry is a running gag in Dublin. Sociologically, the more significant divide is an east-west one: near the bay on either side (east) good; west, generally less so. Thus southeast, the postal district and state of mind called Dublin 4, is reckoned to be best of all.

Tourist Dublin runs on both axes. First, north-south: the central area runs south from Parnell Square along O'Connell Street and across the river, past Trinity and up Grafton Street to St Stephen's Green. On the other axis, it runs west along the quays, past Temple Bar and Christ Church, as far as Heuston Station and the main entrance to the Phoenix Park; and east from St Stephen's Green along Baggot Street, through the heart of the Georgian city, to the Grand Canal and the first of the Dublin 4 suburbs, Ballsbridge.

One-day Special

Morning
Trinity Front Square/Book of Kells

Grafton Street/St Stephen's Green North

Merrion Sq West/Kildare Street/National Museum

Afternoon
Temple Bar

Christ Church/St Patrick's Cathedral

Guinness Storehouse

Four Courts/Custom House

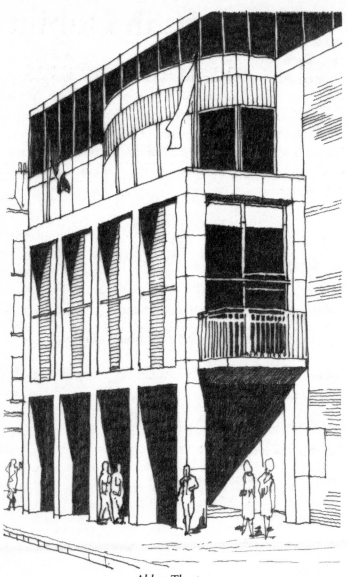

Abbey Theatre

Seven Days in Dublin
Getting Your Bearings

Arrival at the Airport

Dublin Airport is at Collinstown, to the north of the city. The main road to Belfast runs right past it. At the time of writing, Dublin Airport is a bit of a mess. There is rebuilding and expansion in hand with a lot of attendant chaos. Passengers will find that they can have quite long distances to walk to reach baggage reclaim. Once there, if you are unlucky, it can be quite crowded. The exit area through customs and into the arrivals hall is cramped. With luck, this paragraph will be out of date by the time you read it.

There is no rail link to the city centre. You can take public buses run by Dublin Bus, the municipal transport company (routes 16, 16A, 16C, 41, 41B, 41C, 46X, 58X, 746, 747, and 748). All routes will take you to the city centre or direct to Busaras, the central bus station. Some are cross-city routes, also serving some of the southside suburbs. Alternatively, you can take the privately operated Aircoach service which serves a series of locations and hotels in the city centre.

Taxis are available just to the right of the exit from the arrivals hall.

Car hire services are available in the arrivals hall. For the city centre, leave the airport and head down the M1. It has to be admitted that road signage in Dublin is erratic and inconsistent. If you are driving and are not familiar with the city, it is worth spending some time with a city map planning your route. The city is neither enormous nor complicated but you can't rely completely on the signs. This ain't Paris.

Arrival at Ferryport

For foot passengers, the 53A bus serves the city centre. For drivers, there is only one exit from the port. For the city centre, turn left at the exit and proceed along East Wall Road until you reach a little roundabout just short of the East Link Bridge. Do not cross the bridge. Turn right around the roundabout and head along the north quays. This will bring you to Matt Talbot Bridge where the one-way system will take you left across the bridge on to the south side. Turn right along the south quays. George's Quay brings you to Butt Bridge; Burgh Quay to O'Connell Bridge. You are now in the city centre.

For the north city suburbs, turn right out of the port and travel west along East Wall Road. For northeast suburbs, turn right onto Alfie Byrne Road; for all other northside destinations, carry on straight. Remember: signposting in Dublin is erratic, so carry a good road map.

For south city suburbs, cross the East Link toll bridge.

Arrival at Dun Laoghaire

If you are a foot passenger, there is a DART (suburban rail) connection to the city centre or you can take the 46A, 46X or 746 buses.

If you are driving, you can actually trust the road signs. On exiting the terminal, you turn right for the city centre. If you are bound for Dalkey, Killiney, Bray or Wicklow you'll immediately turn left on to York Road and left again on to George's Street. From here, it is straight on for Dalkey and Killiney. For Bray and Wicklow, follow the signs for the N11/M11. For all other routes, follow the directions towards the city centre.

Arrival by Rail

If you are coming from Belfast or Wexford/Rosslare – in effect from anywhere on the east coast of the island – or from Sligo, you'll arrive at Connolly Station in Amiens Street. From here, you are about ten minutes' walk from O'Connell Street. Of course, there are also buses and taxis available. From Galway, Cork, Kerry, Limerick and Waterford-Kilkenny, you'll arrive at Heuston, at the western end of the Liffey quays. This is farther from the city centre, so you'll definitely need to head for the bus stop or the taxi rank.

Essential Information

Tourist Offices

The main Dublin Tourism information office is in St Andrew Street, in the converted church of St Andrew. The main office of Bord Failte-Irish Tourist Board is at Baggot

Street Bridge. There is also a Tourist Information Centre at 12 Upper O'Connell Street.

Transport: Buses, Trains, Taxis

The buses are the workhorses of the city's public transport system. Basically, if you are going to get around by public transport, you'll be on the bus. Their timetables are available on their surprisingly good website, www.dublinbus.ie.

Commuter trains run on a number of lines, of which the coastal DART is the best known. There are also Arrow (outer suburban) services to the west of the city. But large parts of the city's suburban hinterland cannot be accessed by train at all.

Taxis are in the process of being deregulated. Until recently, Dublin taxis were a classic producers' cartel, indifferent to the needs of the public. Now they are offering an increasingly efficient service, although at the time of writing it is still not possible to say how the service will perform at times of greatest demand. This is especially true of the late night taxi service, which has traditionally been a disgrace. Again, one hopes that this observation will just be a bad memory by the time you read this.

Emergencies

The basic emergency telephone numbers are 999 or 112 for fire, police, ambulance, lifeboat and mountain, cave or coastal rescue. The Rape Crisis Centre runs a 24-hour emergency freefone line at 1800 727 737. The Victim Support 24-hour helpline is freefone 1800 661 771.

Post Offices

Not always obvious in the city centre. On the north side, there is the GPO in O'Connell Street, which is very obvious indeed. On the south side, in Andrew Street, across from the Dublin Tourism HQ; in South Anne Street, just off Grafton Street; and – easily missed – in the back of Greene's bookshop in Clare Street, just around the corner from the National Gallery.

All-night Convenience Stores

There are three Centra shops which are open 24 hours: at 36 Upper O'Connell Street; at 15 Lower O'Connell Street; and at 15 Dame Street.

Off-licences

Mitchell's, 21 Kildare Street, is a Dublin institution and is handy for those in the Grafton Street/St Stephen's Green area. Findlater's, Harcourt Street Vaults, in what was once the terminus of the Harcourt Street railway, has a fantastic selection. Oddbins, 17 Upper Baggot St., is a cheerful shop with keenly priced stock: it is part of the popular British chain.

Shoe Repairs

Clegg's, 62 Stephen Street Upper which is just off South Great George's Street. The DART heel bar at 1 Tara Street is just beside the DART station. The Italian Heel Bar, 20 South Anne Street, is just off Grafton Street. O'Connell's, 3 Upper Baggot Street, is handy for those staying on the edge of the city centre.

Luggage Repair

Adamson, 3 Johnson Place, on the curve of the street between South King Street and South William Street, is the best place in town. They sell and repair luggage of all sorts and know all that there is to know about leather goods.

Some of the Best

What follows is a series of personal favourites. There is no attempt to be comprehensive or representative or even fair. Apologies to all who feel unfairly omitted: this section is driven exclusively by personal enthusiasm and experience.

Barber Shop

The Waldorf-Adare, in the basement of 13 Westmoreland Street (phone 677 8608) is a beautifully restored and lovingly minded 1940s-style barber shop. All the classic furniture and fittings, plus free coffee and big-band music on the sound system. And they can cut hair! Liam Finnegan, his daughter Linda and their staff are superb barbers: Linda has won a number of international competitions. Their hot-towel shaves are famous. A lovely place.

Souvenir Shop

The Kilkenny Shop, 6 Nassau Street, has one of the widest selections of quality Irish souvenirs in town. I stress quality: if you want shamrocks, shillelaghs and leprechauns, there are plenty of other places in town for you. The Kilkenny Shop is the place for glassware, pottery, linen and a wide range of other good-quality Irish souvenirs. They are very visitor-friendly and will arrange to ship things if you don't fancy carrying stuff home with you.

Beauty Salon/Foot Massage

Scholl, Grafton Street (6774177) is usually very busy, especially on Saturdays. In summer, however, it may be possible to get a walk-in appointment on weekdays. You should be able to get a walk-in appointment at John Adams at Clery's in O'Connell Street (8173288) or at the Gillian Fox Chiropody Health & Beauty Clinic, 38/39 Morrison Chambers, 32 Nassau Street.

Deli

Magill's, 14 Clarendon Street, is the longest-established delicatessen in Dublin. Salamis and sausages are the most visible product line and contribute most to the shop's marvellous pungent aroma. But this admirable shop sells the full range of deli products: breads, cheeses, olive oil and so on. There are other delis around the town, most of them excellent, but Magill's has been there in bad times as well as good. Worth your custom.

Juice Bar

Nude, 21 Suffolk Street, is the most central juice bar around. Naturally, it has a wide selection of juices to suit all tastes. It also has a mouth-watering selection of wraps to eat in or take away as you choose. Not surprisingly, this is a good (but not exclusively) vegetarian option.

Coffee Shop

Kaffé-Moka, 39 South William Street is just one of a

number of really good coffee shops that have sprung up in recent years. All serve good espresso, cappuccino, latté and so on. In general, as here, the shops tend to be small, intimate and full of young people. A fun place for that essential caffeine fix.

Wine Bar

La Cave, basement 28 South Anne Street, is one of the city's longest-established wine bars. It has atmosphere and a really well-chosen and well-priced selection of wines. They also serve top-class bistro food.

Sandwiches

Panem, at 3 Cope Street in Temple Bar and also at Ha'penny Bridge House, 1 Lower Ormond Quay, which is just across the Millennium Bridge from Temple Bar. Delicious Italian-style sandwiches made on foccacia and ciabatta. Why would anyone want to eat that sad travesty called the traditional sandwich when one can eat like this? Yum yum!

Street Market

Temple Bar market is held every Saturday morning in Meeting House Square. It is becoming something of a Dublin institution for foodies. Breads, cheeses, olives and oils, salamis and meats and lots of other good things. Small by the standards of continental markets but still good fun in one of the city's best new public spaces.

Hand Knits, etc.

Cleo, 18 Kildare Street. Forget about Aran sweaters, this is where to go for really high-quality hand knits and weaves in spectacular colours. A long-established business which has developed into one of the most interesting shops in the city.

Menswear
Kevin & Howlin at 31 Nassau Street specialises in handwoven tweed tailoring for men. Wonderful because it is unique in its single-minded dedication to this old Irish craft tradition, it is a perennial favourite.

Ten Essential Pubs

These are not the ten best pubs in Dublin, although some of them would win a place in that list without difficulty. They are ten personal favourites, designed to give you a cross-section of what the city has to offer. They are indicative, not prescriptive.

Ryan's
of Parkgate Street dates from 1896 and looks much as it did when it opened. The bar is a beautiful semi-circular mahogany counter, with snugs at each end and old brass draught beer pumps. Sadly, the Ryan family sold their interest some years ago and since then standards have slipped fractionally: the television is sometimes turned on and there is piped music. Still, very good hearty pub grub especially at lunchtime and a fine, formal restaurant upstairs. My personal favourite.

Dawson Lounge
Find it yourself: that's half the fun. It is down a spiral staircase in a basement near the Stephen's Green end of

Dawson Street, on the right-hand side as you walk up towards the Green. It is the smallest boozer in the city. Grand little place.

Zanzibar

Theme pubs have been one of the big new things of the last ten years. Mega-bars full of kitschy design and giant screens and throbbing with loud music. The traditional Dublin boozer it most certainly ain't. One of the more successful of this genre is Zanzibar at 34–35 Lower Ormond Quay. The theme, as you may have guessed, is vaguely African. There is nothing subtle or understated here. But it is fun, it is brash, it is alive and it is young. That should do.

Mulligan's of Poolbeg Street

Is this the best pint in town? Many a connoisseur will swear to it. Mulligan's started life as a shebeen in 1782 and has been trading continuously on this site ever since. Low-ceilinged and bearing signs of its antiquity that set it apart from the general run of Victorian pubs — which in much of its décor it resembles — it is a grand, noisy, throbbing boozer when it is full and an oasis of calm when it is not. As for the pint, you must be the judge.

Horseshoe Bar

The smaller of the two public bars in the Shelbourne Hotel, this stylish little gem does not feel like Dublin at all, more like a plush cabin on a cruise ship. That is, until the talk gets lively. Various media celebs and their acolytes like to hang out here. They raise the volume and lower the tone in the most agreeable way.

Doheny & Nesbits

Doheny & Nesbits at 5 Lower Baggot Street gave its name to a school of economists in the 1980s! Just around the corner from Government Buildings, it became a favoured haunt of pundits, politicians, civil servants, advisors, journalists and opinion mongers of every description. It was here, according to the myth, that the booming new Ireland of the Celtic Tiger was first imagined, as the savants drank and debated how the country was to pull itself out of the awful economic mess in which it then found itself. Their influence apparently ran out the door and around the corner into the heart of government. Result: happy ever after. A lovely, traditional dark Dublin boozer.

Porter House

On the corner of Parliament Street and Essex Street East. First and best of the micro-brewery pubs, it serves really good beer. Try a pint of their superb Oyster stout which I am grieved to say puts Guinness in the shade. A well-designed premises on three floors, with pleasant timber décor everywhere, this is a model of the new Dublin pub in every sense of the term. A thoroughly admirable establishment.

Palace Bar

On Fleet Street, near Westmoreland Street, this wonderful pub knocks the socks off most of its rivals in nearby Temple Bar. A simple but beautiful bar room, with a large rectangular lounge at the rear, it was made famous in the 1940s when it was the unofficial editorial office of *The Irish Times* under its then legendary editor Bertie Smyllie. In those years, this was *the* literary pub. It is still one of the best traditional bars in Dublin.

Kehoe's of South Anne Street

One of the pubs nearest to Grafton Street and another of those unspoiled late Victorian drinking shops that are part of the city's glory. Kehoe's is no gin palace, rather a squat, noisy, crowded premises full of life, talk and promise. It is one of those pubs best enjoyed when full (the pub, that is, not you).

O'Neill's of Suffolk Street

Four or five bars in one, with nooks and crannies and interesting corners. O'Neill's is at the centre of Dublin's financial and commercial district and is also the nearest pub to Trinity front gate. So you get a grand mixture of suits, shabby intellectuals and squalid students.

Pubs without Television and Musak

Pubs are for drinking and talking, not for television and musak. A new organisation, the Society for the Protection of Indigenous Noiseless Taverns, or PINT (I know, but it's in a good cause), has been established to maintain some of the traditional boozing decencies. Here are a few pubs that meet with PINT's approval and which you shouldn't miss anyway.

Stag's Head

Just off Exchequer Street at 1 Dame Court, this glorious Victorian gin palace has a politically incorrect stag's head mounted aloft behind the bar. A long bar room is distinguished by mahogany, stained glass and mirrors. Good food is served — traditionally one of the best bacon-and-cabbage venues in town.

Long Hall
Not to be missed. The unprepossessing exterior at 51 South Great George's Street should not deter you. Within, the most sublime collection of kitsch, old prints, geegaws and stuff you ever saw. A genuine original. Gorgeous.

Neary's
A raffish aristocrat in Chatham Street just off the top of Grafton Street. The distinctive twin armatures outside the door mark the spot. A smallish, lived-in bar with a vaguely clubby atmosphere, it provides comfort and ease. This is not a place for the heaving multitudes. The back door gives on to a laneway, on the other side of which is the stage door of the Gaiety theatre. Not good for food.

Peter's Pub
At the top of South William Street, facing down Stephen Street Lower. A small pub, restrained and well mannered, it gets very crowded at busy times, but is a gorgeous little haven in the middle of the afternoon when the rest of this bustling part of town is about its lawful(ish) occasions.

Kavanagh's
Also known (but not to me) as the Gravediggers, this was the last pub in Dublin to serve bottled Guinness which was corked rather than capped — and, yes, you could tell the difference blindfolded. It is in Prospect Square, at the back of Glasnevin Cemetery (see p. 120) and is not easy to find. No pub in Dublin is less changed than this: an authentic old-style drinking shop.

Ten Restaurants

As with the pubs, this is a personal selection and not a definitive guide. It gives an indication of the range of restaurants available in the city. It used to be said — correctly — that Dublin was a grand place in which to be thirsty and a rotten place to be hungry. No more. Eating out is one of the key marks of the new Irish style.

Restaurant Patrick Guilbaud
Guilbaud's, at the Merrion Hotel in Merrion Street, has been the leading restaurant in the city for over a decade. Expensive, not for visitors on a budget but worth every penny. This is a temple of stylish restraint, impeccable service and absolutely outstanding food and wine. If you fancy a splurge, this is where to go.

QV2
14–15 St Andrew Street. The owner-proprietor is a papal count! Johnny McCormack is the grandson of the famous tenor who was given his hereditary gong by Pope Pius XI. This is one of the best mid-market restaurants in town. A pleasant ambience, reliably good food with a slight Cal-Ital feel to it and a well-priced, well-chosen wine list. The name is a reference to a former restaurant here called the Quo Vadis. Highly recommended.

Cooke's Café
On the corner of South William Street and Castle Market. Dearer than QV2, cheaper than Guilbaud's, but very, very good. Again the prevailing inclination is Cal-Ital, but this is

seriously fine cooking served in a pleasant space just across the street from the entrance to the Powerscourt Shopping Centre.

Unicorn
Used to be a venerable Dublin institution, but this restaurant in a lane off Merrion Row has been completely re-made over in recent time, and is now *très chic*. A narrow room, which can leave you a fraction cramped for space, provides a lively buzz especially in the evenings. Prices are on the high side of medium but the food is excellent.

Da Vincenzo
133 Upper Leeson Street. Good pizzas and a solid Italian menu complemented by a decent wine list and friendly service. This is the sort of sensible, neighbourhood-style restaurant that Dublin needs more of. Easy on the pocket and genuinely good value.

Leo Burdock's
2 Werburgh Street. OK, let's cut out the nonsense. Forget all this Celtic Tiger, *nouveau riche* pretension and get back to basics. There are chippers all over the city but Burdock's is by common consent the best. Fish and chips are not an Irish invention. Like so much else, we got them from the English and while it goes hard to say anything good about English food (except their cheeses) you can't deny that a genuine one 'n one is gorgeous. Especially after closing time when you've had a few and it's cold outside. Comfort food. Nobody in Dublin does it better.

Lord Edward

At the corner of Werburgh Street and Christchurch Place, at the top of the pub of the same name. More fish, in a premises next door to Burdock's, but there the resemblance ends. For this is one of the city's longest-established and most expensive fish restaurants. Again, not for those on a budget but genuinely good value none the less. Fish used to be frowned on in Ireland, being associated in people's minds with the Catholic Church's prohibition of meat on Friday. The rediscovery of fish is perhaps the single most heartening development in the recent culinary revolution. The Lord Edward cooks it superbly.

La Boccola

In Meeting House Square in Temple Bar. A splendidly unpretentious trattoria, full of atmosphere and serving good food at affordable prices. Perhaps the best-value Saturday lunch in town, very popular with shoppers weary from the increasingly popular market in the square. This is an establishment that deserves to succeed.

L'Ecrivain

The serious business, at 109a Lower Baggot Street. L'Ecrivain was the restaurateurs' choice as Irish restaurant of the year in 2000. It was always good. Now chef-proprietor Derry Clarke has given the place a total facelift and the stylish new interior is matched by sublime French cooking with Irish ingredients. Outstanding wine list, on which the restaurant does not levy a service charge: a practice, this, which lesser establishments (and that means all but a few restaurants in the city) could usefully follow.

Bang

Almost across the lane from the Unicorn at 11 Merrion Row, this super-stylish café serves beautiful food in a fashionably minimalist setting. Service is efficient and cool, the menu is well thought out and balanced with good vegetarian options and the location is perfect, just off St Stephen's Green and a few doors from the Shelbourne.

Some Things You Can't Do Anywhere Else

Bewley's

A genuine city institution: these wonderful coffee houses are loved by Dubliners. I know that the current owners have turned it into a successful franchise and that you can now go to Bewley's in places like Stansted Airport, for God's sake. And that new ones have been opened all over the suburbs. But there is nothing to beat the real thing: the three original city centre establishments in Westmoreland Street, Grafton Street and South Great George's Street. Every bit as much as the pubs, Bewley's is the heartbeat of the city.

Hurling

This uniquely Irish field sport is one of world's great games. It is a form of field hockey which displays grace, courage and ferocious physical commitment. It is played by two teams of fifteen-a-side; the ball, about the size of a tennis ball but much heavier, is struck with an ash hurley which has a rounded boss on the end; it can also be balanced on the boss by a sprinting player, a skill that never fails to excite the crowd. The object is to strike the ball either under the crossbar (three points) or over it (one point). You can see this lightning-fast game at its best in the summer months of June, July and August in Croke Park, not far from Mountjoy Square. If you decide to go, you won't have any trouble finding your way. Just follow the crowds.

Walk to the Poolbeg Lighthouse

Walk out into the middle of the harbour. The south wall, which encloses the port on one side, runs right down to the distinctive red Poolbeg lighthouse. You get a real sense of the marine location of the city, something that you could very easily miss altogether on a short visit to Dublin. The snag is how to get there. You need a car. Drive across the East Link Bridge to the south side, take the second exit at the roundabout that follows, then the first left. This brings you on to Pigeon House Road, not the most sweet-smelling thoroughfare in Dublin on account of the sewage works nearby! Just follow the road as it swings right under the huge twin chimneys of the electricity generating plant and keep going until you can go no further. From here, you can see the line of the wall running out to the Poolbeg. If you can't get a car, you can always take a taxi but you'll want to be sure that he'll come back for you. Allow 45 minutes to an hour.

Bloomsday

Every 16 June, Joyceans and other well-disposed people like to dress up in Edwardian fig and caper around the town in the footsteps of the immortal Mr Bloom. There are also lectures and other cultural events but the thing is mainly about having fun and celebrating the greatest of all Dublin writers. No city has ever been memorialised as

Dublin was by Joyce. Just watch the newspapers for a list of events or check with the tourist offices.

Gay and Lesbian Dublin

Basically, Dublin is a gay-friendly city and is increasingly popular with gay and lesbian tourists. There is no overt discrimination displayed in bed-and-breakfast establishments or other accommodation venues. Perhaps this is because such discrimination is illegal in Ireland. Violence is no more of a problem for gay people than in any other comparable city, although it is only fair to add that Dublin has nothing to be complacent about where street violence is concerned. Everyone, gay and straight, needs to be on guard late at night when people have drink taken.

The best and quickest fix on the gay and lesbian scene in town can be got from *Gay Community News*, which is available in many outlets in the city centre. Since this book regards Trinity front gate as the umbilicus of the city, you might note that Books Upstairs, 36 College Green, just across the street from front gate, stocks *GCN* on the upstairs balcony. The paper's offices are at 6 South William Street, which also houses the city's Gay & Lesbian Resource Centre (tel. 670 6377). *Gay Commumity News* carries listings of what's on, reviews the club scene and has advertisements for accommodation.

The city's best-established gay pubs are The George, 89 South Great George's Street and The Front Lounge, 33 Parliament Street.

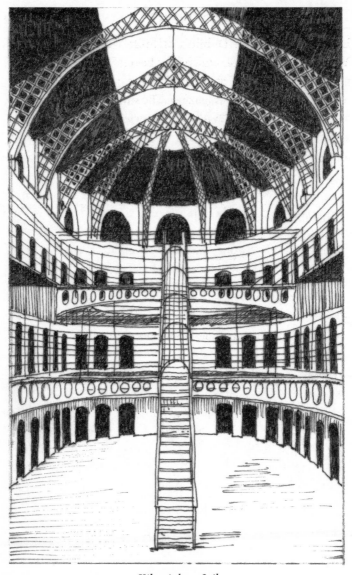

Kilmainham Jail

xxx

Nightlife

Like any other city, Dublin's nightlife is a constant flux. You don't need a book which may be out of date on specific places and venues by the time you read it. You need an up-to-the-minute listings magazine. The simplest thing to do is to buy a copy of *In Dublin*, the city's longest-established guide to all aspects of social life. It is widely available in newsagents.

Top Ten Rainy Day Options

— National Gallery

— National Museum

— Natural History Museum

— Trinity, Book of Kells

— Bank of Ireland, House of Lords

— Christ Church and St Patrick's Cathedrals

— Dublin Castle, including the Chester Beatty Library

— City Hall

— Irish Museum of Modern Art

— Guinness Storehouse

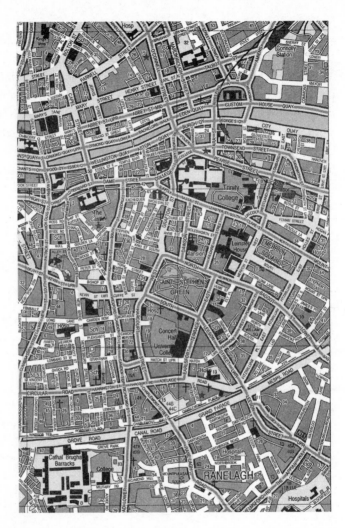

• Trinity • Book of Kells • College Green • Bank of Ireland • Grafton Street • St Stephen's Green • Leeson Street • Harcourt Street • South Great George's Street • Fitzwilliam Square • Government Buildings Merrion Square • Upper Mount Street • National Gallery • Kildare Street • Leinster House • National Library • National Museum • Molesworth Street

Day 1

Trinity and the Georgian City

Day 1 Teaser

Her nom de plume was Hope. Who was she?

Trinity

Start at Trinity College. In *Ulysses*, Joyce refers to 'Trinity's surly front'. Joyce was not a Trinity man and had no particular reason to love the College of the Holy & Undivided. For all that, 'surly' is hardly the *mot juste*. This is a splendid classical façade, facing College Green (which is no longer a green and does not contain as much as a blade of grass) and Dame Street.

Trinity is the only college of the University of Dublin, a foundation established by Queen Elizabeth I in 1592 to promote 'learning, civility and true religion' among the Irishry. The reference to true religion meant that Trinity was a Protestant (Anglican variety) establishment from the start. So it remained, more or less, until the second half of the twentieth century. A rival Catholic university (Joyce's alma mater and the source of his sourness towards Trinity) was finally established in 1854; after a number of name changes it became University College Dublin (UCD). It occupies a suburban campus in Belfield in the farther reaches of Dublin 4. You can go out there on the number 10 bus.

Until the 1970s, the Catholic archbishop of Dublin — an acidulous old rigorist called John Charles McQuaid — actually forbade Catholics to attend Trinity without his specific permission, which was seldom if ever granted. Few among the faithful defied the ban, which left Trinity rather light on students. Once the ban went out, the numbers went up and the place is now bursting at the seams. Because of its fantastic location in the heart of the city and the cachet flowing from its antiquity, it is now *the* centre of student fashion in Dublin.

Trinity is open to the public without let or hindrance. Go in past the twin statues of Oliver Goldsmith and Edmund Burke — two of Trinity's most distinguished alumni — the work of the fine Irish Victorian sculptor John Henry Foley. Pass under the canopy of Regent House. This brings you into Parliament Square, so called because much of what you see here was paid for by the old colonial parliament which sat on the far side of College Green, in what is now the Bank of Ireland (of which more anon). It is more commonly called Front Square. The contrast with the bustle of College Green, barely 50 metres behind you, is total. Here is classical control and order, the harmonious arrangement of individual buildings to form a balanced unity.

The reverse façade of Regent House is a mirror image of the West Front facing College Green. It dates from the 1750s and is variously attributed to Henry Keene and John

Front Square Trinity College

Sanderson and to Theodore Jacobsen. On either side are the symetrically colonnaded fronts of the Chapel (left as you stand with your back to the college entrance) and the Examination Hall, both designed by Sir William Chambers in the late eighteenth century. Chambers, who never set a foot in Ireland, also designed Charlemont House (now the Hugh Lane Municipal Gallery) in Parnell Square (p. 95) and the Casino at Marino (p.122). In every case, he simply sent the plans over from London, where he was one of the most fashionable architects of the day: Somerset House in the Strand is his masterpiece.

Tucked in behind the chapel is the Dining Hall, designed by Richard Castle and dating from 1743. It was restored in the 1980s following a disastrous fire, although happily the food at Commons remains as bad as ever. Facing it, and recessed behind the Examination Hall, is the curious little Science Reading Room of 1937.

Stand in the middle of Front Square taking all this in. The view directly before you is dominated by the Campanile or bell tower of 1853. Most Dubliners have never heard the Campanile bells peal. A joke has it that they ring spontaneously whenever a female virgin undergraduate walks beneath them, an event last recorded in 1909. This joke is especially popular out in UCD. The Campanile is flanked by statues of George Salmon, provost of Trinity from 1888 to 1904 ('tinned salmon' in *Ulysses*) and William Hartpole Lecky, the great historian. Behind it, on the manicured lawn, is Henry Moore's *Reclining Connected Forms* (1969).

From here, it is best to go clockwise round college. On your left beyond the Dining Hall is the Graduates' Memorial Building (GMB), a fine Victorian confection. Behind it, and bounded by Pearse Street, lies the area of college known as Botany Bay because the original college gardens stood here. Passing the front of the GMB brings us to the Rubrics, the oldest surviving building in Trinity. It dates from about 1700, is built in the red brick style (hence the name) known in Dublin as Dutch Billy, after King William III, the Prince of Orange whose successful *coup d'etat* in 1688 is still quaintly referred to in Britain as the Glorious Revolution.

The back of the Rubrics encloses the west side of New Square. To your left is the curious little Printing House (1732) also by Richard Castle. The rather undistinguished buildings on the north and east sides of New Square are occupied by college offices and rooms but the south side is worth a second glance. This is the Museum Building, built in 1853 in the then fashionable Victorian Venetian style. The architects were Thomas Deane and Benjamin Woodward, who were influenced by Ruskin's *Stones of Venice*: Ruskin so liked this building that he brought Deane and Woodward to Oxford to build the museum there.

Leave New Square at the southeast corner (in other words, at the far diagonal to where we entered), walk past a small ornamental garden and you find yourself in the College Park. There is just one piece of advice here: stop and sit down. This is one of the most pleasant spaces in the city, especially in fine summer weather. If you are lucky, there will be a cricket match in progress and you can watch this hypnotic, soporific and completely incomprehensible ritual until your eyelids begin to droop.

When you come to, retrace your steps to New Square and walk along the south side past the Museum Building. This brings you to Paul Koralek's Berkeley Library (1967), a splendidly uncompromising piece of modernity. Walk along the forecourt past Arnaldo Pomodoro's intriguing sculpture *Sphere and Sphere* (1987). Rather than entering the library, turn right and debouch into Fellows' Square. Stop. On your left is the Arts block, also by Koralek (1978), a fine piece of infill on a narrow site — although less successful internally than externally (given its sensitive location, that is the better choice). Straight ahead at the far end of Fellows' Square is the Provost's Garden and House, the front of which gives on to Grafton Street. The sculpture in the middle of the square is *Cactus* by Alexander Calder (1967).

The building to your right is the Old Library. Completed in 1732 to the design of Thomas Burgh, it is the epicentre of tourist Trinity. First of all, it is very beautiful. The oak barrel-vaulted ceiling in the Long Room — not part of Burgh's original design, but a later Victorian addition by Deane and Woodward — is particularly dramatic. The Library also houses the Dublin Experience, a 45-minute audiovisual history of the city, the manuscripts known as the Book of Durrow and the Book of Armagh, a couple of old Irish harps and many other treasures. But all of this pales beside the *Book of Kells*, which is why you are really here.

The Book of Kells is an illuminated manuscript. That means simply that it is a handwritten text with rich coloured decorations in the form of illustrations, elaborate designs and decorated capital letters. The text is a Latin translation of the Four Gospels. It was found in the County Meath town of Kells — a celebrated Columban monastic site — but was probably composed on the island of Iona in the Inner Hebrides where St Columba (Columcille in the Irish spelling) had his principal monastery.

The Book of Kells is probably the most famous illuminated manuscript in the world. It is the supreme surviving work of art from the heroic age of early Irish Christianity. It has been in the safe keeping of Trinity since the seventeenth century and is kept in carefully controlled conditions of temperature and humidity: one two-page opening is displayed each day.

When you exit the Old Library, you have a choice. You can leave college via the Arts Block which leads directly into Nassau Street at the end of Dawson Street. This has the advantage of taking you past the Douglas Hyde Gallery in the Arts Block, which hosts exhibitions of contemporary art. Alternatively, you can go around the corner back into Front Square and leave by Front Gate, where you came in. This is the route we follow here.

FAMOUS TRINITY GRADUATES

William Congreve (1670–1729), dramatist, author of *The Way of the World*.

Jonathan Swift (1667–1745), the greatest satirist in the English language, author of *Gulliver's Travels*.

George Farquhar (1678–1707), dramatist, author of *The Recruiting Officer* and *The Beaux' Stratagem*.

George Berkeley (1685–1753), immaterialist philosopher, author of *A Treatise Concerning the Principles of Human Knowledge*.

Oliver Goldsmith (1728–74), writer, author of *The Vicar of Wakefield* and *She Stoops to Conquer*.

Edmund Burke (1729–97), writer and political philosopher, author of *Reflections on the Revolution in France*, father of modern British Conservatism.

Richard Lovell Edgeworth (1744–1817), inventor, polymath and eccentric, founder-member of the Royal Irish Academy and father of Maria Edgeworth, the novelist.

Henry Grattan (1746–1820), leader of the liberal faction in the Anglo-Irish colonial parliament and opponent of the Act of Union.

Theobald Wolfe Tone (1763–98), revolutionary and charming opportunist, the father of Irish republicanism.

Robert Emmet (1778–1803), revolutionary *naif*, the 'darlin' of Erin', hanged for organising the botched insurrection of 1803, remembered for his speech from the dock.

The O'Gorman Mahon (1800–91), adventurer, rogue, philanderer and politician, he was variously an officer in the Russian imperial bodyguard, a general in the Uruguayan army, an admiral in the Chilean navy, a colonel of chasseurs under Napoleon III and at various times in between MP for Clare.

William Rowan Hamilton (1805–65) mathematician, author of *The Elements of Quaternions*.

John Mitchel (1815–75), Young Irelander, journalist and author. His *Jail Journal* a classic of its kind. Not one of nature's moderates, he supported the Confederacy in the US civil war.

Joseph Sheridan Le Fanu (1814–73), Gothic novelist, author of *The House by the Churchyard*, and editor-proprietor of *Dublin University Magazine*.

Thomas Davis (1814–45), idealistic leader of the Young Ireland movement, a huge influence on later nationalists.

Nathaniel Hone (1831–1917), painter, one of a prolific artistic family and among the first Irish artists influenced by the French Barbizon school which anticipated Impressionism.

Edward Carson (1854–1935), lawyer and politician, leader of the Ulster Unionists in resisting home rule and nemesis of Oscar Wilde.

Oscar Wilde (1854–1900), dramatist and supreme wit, author of *The Importance of Being Earnest*.

Percy French (1854–1920), popular song writer who wrote 'The Mountains of Mourne' and other sentimental and witty ballads.

Douglas Hyde (1860–1949), scholar and first President of

the Republic of Ireland, he was the founding father of the Gaelic League and a critical figure in the Irish cultural renaissance around 1900.

John Millington Synge (1871–1909), dramatist, author of *The Playboy of the Western World.*

Oliver St John Gogarty (1878–1957), surgeon, wit and minor poet, the model for Buck Mulligan in Joyce's *Ulysses.*

Ernest Walton (1903–95), scientist and winner of the Nobel Prize for Physics in 1951.

Samuel Beckett (1906–89), dramatist and winner of the Nobel Prize for Literature in 1969, author of *Waiting for Godot.*

Vivian Mercier (1919–89), literary critic who wrote The *Irish Comic Tradition* and famously summarised Beckett's *Godot* as 'a play in which nothing happens, twice'.

College Green

Stand with your back to Trinity. You are now facing west onto College Green and Dame Street. On your right is the **Bank of Ireland** — no longer its head office, merely a branch. But what a branch! It was originally built as the parliament house for the old pre-Act of Union Irish parliament. An Irish parliament of some sort had existed since the thirteenth century but, as with much else in Dublin, it was not until the eighteenth century that its fortunes really waxed. It moved to this site in the 1730s, when this wonderful building — designed by Sir Edward Lovett Pearce — was completed.

It was a colonial parliament, similar to the pre-independence assemblies in America. Like them, it was representative of the colonial élite only: the Anglican ascendancy which represented about one in ten of the population of eighteenth-century Ireland. It housed the Lords and Commons of the Kingdom of Ireland, a kingdom which in theory was separate from that of Britain, although sharing a common monarch. This was a polite fiction, all very well in constitutional theory but fatally flawed as events were to prove in 1800. However, when it was new, the parliament house was a testimony to the sense of solidity and self-confidence felt by the Ascendancy after the turmoil and wars of the previous century.

Pearce's original building was later added to by James Gandon and Robert Parke. Gandon, the greatest of eighteenth-century Dublin architects, designed the colonnaded extension around the corner into Westmoreland Street which provided a ceremonial entrance to the House of Lords.

It all ended in tears. The old parliament could not reform itself and remained stubbornly wedded to the privileges of the élite which it represented. The gilded world of the eighteenth-century ascendancy did not survive the pressures flowing from France following the revolution. Britain itself was drawn into war with France from 1793; five years later, the Rising of 1798 erupted in the name of a wholly new concept: that of a secular Irish republic independent of Britain. London could not possibly tolerate such a thing at her back door in time of war (or of peace). No longer trusting the colonial élite to govern Ireland in Britain's interest, Pitt's government persuaded the Irish parliament to liquidate itself. It required a small fortune in bribes to get the job done, but done it was. Under the Act of Union of 1801, the parliament ceased to exist and Ireland was henceforth to be governed from Westminster, just like England, Scotland and Wales. That remained the position until 1922.

The 'old house in College Green' became the focus of all nineteenth-century nationalists who wished to repeal the union and establish home rule. But in 1802 the building was sold to the Bank of Ireland for £40,000. It was a condition of the sale that the old House of Commons be gutted, which it duly was. Happily, however, the House of Lords was left alone and still stands today as it did when the Lords Norbury, Donoghmore, Blessington and all the rest of the eighteenth-century grandees were in their pomp. It is open to visitors during normal banking hours. The wonderful chandelier dates from 1788 and the two huge tapestries celebrate the Protestant victories of the Siege of Derry (1689) and the Battle of the Boyne (1690) which laid the basis for the ascendancy's security in its century of ease.

The late eighteenth-century parliament is often referred to as Grattan's Parliament, after Henry Grattan (1746–1820), its most liberal and eloquent member. His statue — by John Henry Foley — stands facing Trinity. Farther up College Green, almost in Dame Street, is Edward Delany's statue of the mid nineteenth-century patriot Thomas Davis.

Grafton Street

Grafton Street connects College Green to St Stephen's Green and is the last part of that central north-south axis mentioned in the 'Get Orientated' section. It is Dublin's most fashionable shopping street, although coarsened in recent years by some British chain stores, fast-food joints and sportsgear shops. Still, there is something indomitable about it. 'Grafton Street gay with housed awnings lured his senses. Muslin prints, silk, dames and dowagers, jingle of harnesses, hoofthuds lowringing in the baking causeway' was how Leopold Bloom found it at lunchtime on 16 June 1904.

No. 1 Grafton Street, on the left as you go up and before you enter the principal part of the street beyond the Nassau Street-Suffolk Street intersection, is the front of the Provost's House in Trinity. It is the only one of the monumental town houses built in the eighteenth century still serving its original purpose. On the right, close to the corner of College Green, are two celebrated premises selling pipes, tobacco and other requisites. These are Fox's and Kapp & Petersen's and by some miracle they have so far avoided the contumely of the anti-tobacco fascists.

Farther up on the right, near the Suffolk Street corner, there is a statue representing the mythical Molly Malone. She was a fishmonger about whom Dublin's signature ballad was written. According to the lyric, she expired of the fever. The statuesque [sic] creature in Grafton Street does not look at all feverish; in fact, she looks like a Baywatch wannabe in the whole of her health.

Cross the junction into the main part of the street. Weir's, on the corner of Wicklow Street, is the largest jewellers in the city. On the opposite corner is Brown Thomas, the city's leading department store. It used to stand across the street but it swallowed its former rival Switzer's, whose old premises it now occupies, and sold its lovely shop across the street to Marks & Spencer, as if there were not enough uniformity in the world. Brown Thomas is a bland, expensive, international-type department store. It's grand, but it could be anywhere.

Which is not something you can say of Bewley's, a little farther on. Bewley's Oriental Café is a city institution. It is an old-fashioned coffee house, Dublin's social exchange, a place to meet, chat, hide, relax, whatever (see section 'Some Things You Can't Do Anywhere Else'). You will find as good a cross-section of Dublin life within as anywhere else in the city. People from all arts and parts gather here. It is not that the food is exceptional — anything but — although the coffee is reasonable and the cakes and sticky buns are part of the ritual. It is just — the place: 'the lofty, rackety café' with its booths and banquettes, its chinoiserie, its stained glass and its odd combination of clatter and calm. Of course, it is not the same since it went self-service (although there is still waitress service in the small upstairs room). Part of its charm is that, like the pint of Guinness, persons beyond a certain age can moan about how much better it was in the old days while still enthusiastically consuming the modern product.

Just beside Bewley's is Johnson's Court, a charming lane that connects with Clarendon Street.

Bewley's Café, Grafton Street

The rest of Grafton Street contains the usual mixture of shops you would expect in a street like this. On the left, near the top of the street, watch out for Captain America's Cookhouse, which dates from 1971 and was the first American-style restaurant in Dublin. Noisy, vulgar and perfectly fine — especially for kids — it has had many imitators and few rivals. It also has a licence, the only premises on the whole street where you can get a jar. However, don't panic: there are oodles of boozers in the streets adjacent.

St Stephen's Green

The top of Grafton Street brings you to St Stephen's Green. It has been an enclosed space since the 1660s but was not opened to the public until the 1880s thanks to the munificence of the owner, Lord Ardilaun, the then head of the Guinness family.

As you emerge from Grafton Street, you are on the northwest corner of the Green. The best way to see the square which encloses the Green proper is to cross over to the railings and walk around clockwise, proceeding in turn along the north, east, south and west sides to return to your starting point.

The north side has always been the most fashionable. In the eighteenth century, it was known as Beaux Walk, being the place where people of style, wealth and fashion used to promenade in an Anglo-Irish version of the *passeggiata*. Between Grafton Street and the corner of Dawson Street are the United Services Club and the Stephen's Green Club, both members only. Between Dawson Street and Kildare

Street, at number 17, is the University and Kildare Street Club, likewise private, and the product of a merger between what had traditionally been two of the city's more pluterperfectly Protestant institutions. The University Club was established for Trinity graduates in the days when Catholics hardly attended, whereas the Kildare Street Club — originally housed in a fine Deane & Woodward building at the end of Kildare Street — was the spiritual home of florid, bewhiskered Irish Tories.

The northeast corner of the Green is dominated by the fine Shelbourne Hotel, which still has the best location of all the top-class hotels in town. It faces the east side, which is the route we now take. As we turn the corner of the Green, we pass Edward Delany's impressive memorial to Wolfe Tone, the eighteenth-century republican. For reasons that will be clear when you see it, it is known to Dubliners — who still possess that glib facility for snide wit that so enraged Bernard Shaw — as Tonehenge. Shaw regarded this sort of thing as symptomatic of the city's failure and futility: he could be a very funny man when he chose but, like many self-improvers, he could also be a humourless prig.

The first side street opposite is Hume Street. You will notice that the buildings on this corner are fairly obviously pastiche Georgian rather than the real thing. The real thing had survived until the late 1960s when developers got their hands on it. The threatened demolition resulted in the first major environmental protest in modern Ireland, as architectural students occupied the site to protest at the wanton destruction of the city's heritage. It is hard to credit it now, but there were some people — not all of them mere property developers but even some otherwise respectable people high up in Irish life — who regarded the destruction of Georgian Dublin as a good thing. You see, it had been built by the Anglo-Irish (for that read 'English') ascendancy in the eighteenth century and was therefore the work of the colonial oppressor. In the end, the compromise you see settled the matter to nobody's satisfaction, although it could have been a lot worse.

You see why at the next corner when you turn on to the south side of the Green. From the corner of Earlsfort Terrace, the first three buildings along are fine examples of 1960s dreck, such as might now be polluting the corner of Hume Street. The last of these perfectly undistinguished office blocks is home to the Department of Justice.

A little farther on, however, we come to Iveagh House, which is very distinguished indeed and houses the Department of Foreign Affairs. It dates from 1736 and was owned for many years by the Guinness family (Iveagh is one of the many lordly titles the family acquired over the years) who presented it to the nation in 1939.

Number 86 is Newman House, site of the original Catholic University (1854), the lineal antecedent of UCD. There is an irony here, for number 86 was originally built in 1765 for Richard Whaley, a robustly Protestant gentleman whose dislike of Catholicism earned him the sobriquet 'Burnchapel Whaley'. His son Thomas, better known as Buck Whaley, was one of the most rakish men-about-town in the late eighteenth century. A spendthrift, he flew through his inheritance before repairing his fortune in the most spectacular way. He won a bet — reputedly for

£20,000 — by travelling from Dublin to Jerusalem and back in less than two years. In 1908, the college moved around the corner to what is now the National Concert Hall in Earlsfort Terrace, before relocating to far suburban Belfield in 1970. It was here, however, in number 86, that Joyce studied. It is this building which is the setting for the final chapter of *A Portrait of the Artist as a Young Man*. Newman House is still owned by UCD.

Beside it is a little gem, University Church, a small mock-Byzantine chapel founded by Cardinal Newman in 1854 during his time as first president of the Catholic University. It was designed by John Hungerford Pollen. The Byzantine style had a vogue among some Catholic church builders in the nineteenth century, its lavish ornamentation, mosaics and iconography a vivid contrast to the austerity of Protestant churches. Perhaps the best — certainly the biggest — example in these islands is Westminster Cathedral in London, the supreme symbol of Catholic renewal in the heart of the English capital. University Church expresses a similar exuberant assertion of architectural values which mirror the liturgical theatricality of Catholicism.

The west side of St Stephen's Green has always been the least fashionable. There used to be a gallows here in the seventeenth and eighteenth centuries and one supposes that it did not do much for the neighbourhood. To this day, the visitor can see that this side of the Green gives into side streets that are visibly less stylish and elegant than the other three sides. The west side is dominated by the premises of the Royal College of Surgeons in Ireland, dating from

1805. Farther on, at the corner of Grafton Street and South King Street, stands the Stephen's Green Shopping Centre.

By now, we have completed our circuit of the square that encloses the Green. It is, incidentally, the largest square in Dublin and one of the largest urban squares in Europe. Time now to enter the Green itself. The entrance takes us under the Memorial Arch to the officers and men of the Royal Dublin Fusiliers who fell in the Boer War, 1899–1902.

This is Dublin's best loved public park. It contains two pleasing artificial lakes, ducks and other wildfowl to beat the band, a children's playground, a garden for the blind, a bandstand, lots of neat municipal flower beds and statues to James Joyce, Tom Kettle (a contemporary of Joyce who died in the Great War) and Yeats, among others. The latter is particularly fine, being a Henry Moore set in a recessed grotto area near the centre of the Green. Near the southeast entrance, at the corner nearest to Leeson Street and Earlsfort Terrace, is a fountain called the Three Fates, a gift from Germany to Ireland acknowledging the Irish contribution to the relief of distress and destruction in Germany following the Second World War. But mostly, the Green is all about lolling about, relaxing, chilling out, taking your ease. Sit down; feed the ducks; smell the flowers.

OPTIONS OFF THE GREEN

Leeson St./Earsfort Terrace/Hatch St./Harcourt St.

The main section of this itinerary takes us along the north side of the Green and into Merrion Row. However, there are other options for those with extra time to spare. From the southeast corner of the Green, Lower Leeson Street runs all the way up to the Grand Canal; on the far side of the canal bridge, it becomes Upper Leeson Street before melting into Morehampton Road, which is the start of the suburb of Donnybrook. Leeson Street is Georgian, as is much of the surrounding area. At the junction with Fitzwilliam Place, just before you reach the canal bridge, stop. The view to your left takes in the longest unbroken (almost) Georgian vista in the city, along the line of Fitzwilliam Place, Fitzwilliam Square East, Fitzwilliam Street Upper and Lower and Merrion Square East. It is enclosed at the far end by the National Maternity Hospital. That parenthetical 'almost' refers to the premises of the Electricity Supply Board in Fitzwilliam Street Lower, of which more anon.

The stretch of the Grand Canal from Leeson Street bridge left down as far as Baggot Street Bridge is very pleasant. The towpath takes you past the memorial to the poet Patrick Kavanagh (see cover photograph).

Back on Leeson Street, about half way between Stephen's Green and the canal bridge, there is a junction. Pembroke Street on one side leads into Fitzwilliam Square. Take the opposite turn, which brings you along Hatch Street. You cross Earlsfort Terrace, passing the National Concert Hall.

It was originally built to house the international exhibition of 1865, and was then rebuilt when UCD took it over after 1909. UCD moved out – except for one or two minor faculties which are still here – in the 1970s and the building was further converted for use as the concert hall, in which capacity it opened in 1981. It filled a yawning gap in the city's cultural life.

Walk along the rest of Hatch Street to the junction with Harcourt Street. On the left-hand corner is the rear wall of what was originally Harcourt Street Station, the terminus of a suburban rail line which was closed in 1959. Contrary to legend, there were hardly any protests at the time. Later on, it seemed like a woefully short-sighted decision when the roads from the southern suburbs were choked with commuter cars every morning and evening. One of the most famous Irish railway photographs shows a steam engine which crashed through this wall in 1900. Its brakes had failed on the approach to the station and it careered right through the buffers, ending up with its front section sticking out into Hatch Street.

Turn right into Harcourt Street, a fine curving Georgian street dating from the 1770s. Number 17 was originally called Clonmell House. It was built for a man called John Scott, a shyster lawyer who made a fortune at the Bar and ended his days as Viscount Clonmell, chief justice of Ireland (although known to one and all as 'Copper-faced Jack'). His neighbour at No. 14 was another slippery barrister but a vastly more likeable one. Sir Jonah Barrington was the author of a number of books, of which the *Personal Sketches of His Own Time* is the best loved and best remembered. Deservedly so, for it is one of the most amusing — if not always reliable — accounts we have of the late eighteenth-century Ascendancy. Barrington was merely a rogue — unlike Clonmell who was a swindler and a crook — with a talent for tall tales. He opposed the Act of Union of 1800, but not before accepting a handsome government bribe to support it. He was granted a knighthood and appointed a judge but he was hopeless with money and was constantly in debt. Anyone reading the *Personal Sketches* can guess why: for all his faults, he was a generous-hearted, life-affirming, bibulous old party, not a man to reckon the pennies. Eventually, he solved his financial problems at a stroke by peculating money lodged in his court. He legged it to Paris — where else? — never to return.

Number 6 was the original premises of the Gaelic League, founded by Douglas Hyde in 1893 with the aim of 'de-anglicising Ireland', an ambition not to the liking of Edward Carson, the barrister and leader of Ulster unionist resistance to home rule, who had been born in No. 4.

The northern end of Harcourt Street returns you to St Stephen's Green.

Between Grafton St and South Great Georges' Street
The other variable option for those with a little time to spare is to explore the series of streets between the top of Grafton Street and South Great George's Street. Start outside the Stephen's Green Shopping Centre and walk down South King Street. The main interest lies in the Gaiety Theatre on the right-hand side, a fine old Victorian

music hall dating from 1871. It is now used variously as a straight theatre, a variety theatre, a Christmas pantomime venue and, most improbably, an opera house. It hosts Opera Ireland's twice-yearly seasons of grand opera. The city, to its shame, still has no dedicated music theatre where musicals, operetta and grand opera can be properly staged.

This is an area for mooching about. I suggest the following route: right at the end of South King Street into South William Street; straight across the Exchequer Street–Wicklow Street intersection into Andrew Street which in turn curves right into Suffolk Street. Turn right up Grafton Street as far as the first right, which is Wicklow Street. Take the first left into Clarendon Street and the first right into Coppinger Row. Cross South William Street into Castle Market; turn left into Drury Street and right into Fade Street. This brings you onto South Great George's Street. Turn right. You can take either of the next two right-hand turns. The first is Market Arcade; if you take this it brings you back to Drury Street opposite Castle Market, in which case you go left down to Exchequer Street, where you turn right. The second right off George's Street, at the corner of the Central Hotel, is Exchequer Street. You turn right into it, passing the end of Drury Street where the Market Arcade option would have brought you, and from here carry on straight, re-entering Wicklow Street before finishing in Grafton Street.

Places to watch out for along the way, in the order of the itinerary above, are:

Georgian Doorway

- Dublin Civic Museum, on the corner of South William Street and Coppinger Row. A splendidly eclectic collection of Dublin memorabilia, this homely, unpretentious and charming museum is a personal favourite.

- Powerscourt Townhouse Centre, a few doors along, dominates South William Street. It is a shopping centre and as these places go, it has some style. It was originally built in 1774 as the town house of the Lords Powerscourt, using granite quarried from their Co. Wicklow estate. It was sold to the government in 1807 — typical of the flight of wealth and fashion from the city in the years following the Union — and from the 1830s until 1981 it was the headquarters of a wholesale warehouse company. It is good to see this fine lump of a building employed as a public space, contributing to the life of the city.

- Dublin Tourism headquarters is in the converted St Andrew's church in the street of the same name. The statue of St Andrew in the old churchyard is badly corroded by weather. It originally stood over the entrance door. In this position, it was on a direct line of fire from Daly's Club on College Green, the most fashionable gaming house in the city in the late eighteenth century. The bucks from Daly's used to amuse themselves by taking pot shots at St Andrew with their pistols. Those old boys really knew how to knock out a good time.

- St Teresa's Church, Clarendon Street, built in 1793 for the Discalced Carmelites, was one of the first city-centre Catholic churches built following the end of the Penal Laws which discriminated in various ways against Catholics (and also against Protestant dissenters). It has a side entrance which gives into the charming Johnson's Court.

- The South City Markets, between South Great George's Street and Drury Street, date from 1881. The far side of South Great George's Street is defaced by one of the worst buildings in the city (and that is saying something). Standing on the site of Pim's, one of the city's old Edwardian department stores, it is a brutal, horizontal intrusion into what is otherwise a coherent, red-brick Victorian street. Architecturally, the 1960s and 1970s were a disaster for Dublin. This piece of dreck is occupied for the most part by government functionaries.

The Georgian Squares

The route to what is the heart of the Georgian city starts on the north side of St Stephen's Green. Walk along past the Shelbourne Hotel and into Merrion Row. The little Huguenot Cemetery on your left dates from 1693 and has been lovingly restored in recent years after decades of neglect. It recalls a community that gave much to the city. Many Huguenots (French Protestants) fled France following the Revocation of the Edict of Nantes in 1685. The edict had been the central feature of religious tolerance following the sixteenth-century wars of religion. Huguenots settled in various parts of Britain and Ireland: Dublin was a natural destination, being a preponderantly

Protestant city at the time. Note, however, the misspelling of the word 'Huguenot' over the gate, the most conspicuously public piece of illiteracy in the city.

At the first junction along, it is worth a detour into Ely Place on the right. It is a cul de sac. Many famous and infamous people lived here. Number 6 was the home of 'Black Jack' Fitzgibbon, Lord Clare, the hated promoter of the Act of Union. His funeral cortege in 1802 was pelted with dead cats by the Dublin mob. Number 4 was the home of Clare's contemporary, the great barrister John Philpot Curran, a liberal and reckoned the wittiest and most eloquent man in Dublin, a fair old boast in any age. Later it was home to the novelist George Moore, whose mordant trilogy *Hail and Farewell* is one of the great Dublin autobiographies. The Gallagher Gallery of the Royal Hibernian Academy occupies the right-hand end of Ely Place and is generally worth a visit.

Note for British visitors: In Dublin, it is pronounced Ee-lie (rhymes with 'belie') not Ee-ly (rhymes with 'touchy-feely'). Strange, but there you go.

Return to Merrion Row and turn right towards Baggot Street. Take the first right into Lower Pembroke Street which brings you into **Fitzwilliam Square**.

The Viscounts Fitzwilliam of Merrion were the greatest property developers in late eighteenth-century and early nineteenth-century Dublin. No family has left a deeper or a more benign thumbprint on the city. They developed almost all of the Georgian city between St Stephen's Green and the Grand Canal including Merrion and Fitzwilliam Squares,

Baggot Street, Mount Street Upper and Lower and all the surrounding and connecting streets. The Fitzwilliam family line died out in 1816 and the estate passed to the Earls of Pembroke (family surname Herbert), who continued the development of the area. Any place name containing the words Merrion, Fitzwilliam, Pembroke or Herbert is part of their development. A glance at a map will suffice to register the sheer scale of what they did.

Fitzwilliam Square was not completed until the 1820s and is therefore a relatively late arrival. However, the marvellous unity of this whole area renders the chronology of construction fairly unimportant. Fitzwilliam is the smallest of the city's Georgian squares and the only one in which the central garden is still reserved for keyholders. Starting on the west side you can wander into Upper Pembroke Street or around the square itself.

Leave by Upper Fitzwilliam Street. (Incidentally, if you are confused by all this upper and lower stuff, it is simple: the lower part of a street is that part nearest to the mouth of the Liffey.) Number 3 is the premises of the United Arts Club, of which W.B. Yeats was a founder-member. Turn left into Baggot Street, averting your gaze, if you can, from the Electricity Supply Board's office block on the far right diagonal in Lower Fitzwilliam Street. A mere sixteen Georgian houses were knocked to make way for this masterpiece. To be fair, it could be worse: it is not completely unsympathetic to its position but even if it were a better building, it is still in the wrong place. Something unique was destroyed to accommodate something commonplace.

Happily, our route takes us away from it. Walk along Baggot Street back towards the junction of Merrion Row and Ely Place-Merrion Street. Then turn right into Merrion Street, which leads to **Merrion Square**.

The large complex on the left is **Government Buildings**. It dates from 1911 and was originally the Royal College of Science. It was thoroughly overhauled and modernised by Charles Haughey when he was Taoiseach (prime minister). The terrace of houses directly across the street includes Mornington House, No. 24, birthplace of Arthur Wellesley, Duke of Wellington, victor at Waterloo and greatest of British generals. It is now part of the Merrion Hotel.

Just on the edge of Merrion Square West is the Natural History Museum, part of the complex that includes the **National Gallery** down the street and the **National Museum** and **National Library** on the far side of the block in Kildare Street. The Natural History Museum is a gem. It is wondrously quaint. It is also wondrously interesting. The collection principally comprises examples of Irish fauna, although the first floor also has a family of gorillas, all expertly stuffed, which are a testimony to the collecting instincts of the members of the Royal Dublin Society under whose aegis the museum originally came. I once heard a young girl, one of a school party who were gazing with undisguised awe at the alpha male, say: 'Jaysis, his tings aren't even widdered!'

Back outside, we are in Merrion Square. On the west side, which we are now on, the Natural History Museum is separated from the National Gallery down the street by

Leinster Lawn which is the back of **Leinster House,** seat of the Dáil and Seanad (lower and upper houses of parliament). Stand with your back to Leinster Lawn and look along the south side of the square. I know that it is a cliché, but this is *the* Dublin view. You are looking along Merrion Square South, across the junction of Lower Fitzwilliam Street and along **Upper Mount Street.** The view is enclosed by the Church of St Stephen at Mount Street Crescent, known to all Dubliners as the Pepper Canister church.

I suggest that you walk along Merrion Square South and head straight for the Pepper Cannister. The houses that you pass on the Square have many historic associations. In the order that you pass them, George Russell (AE), the writer, mystic and champion of the co-operative movement, worked at No. 84; W.B. Yeats lived for a while at No. 82; No. 70, now the headquarters of the Arts Council, was the home of the gothic novelist Joseph Sheridan Le Fanu; Daniel O'Connell, the patriot, lived at No. 58.

Merrion Square is divided from Upper Mount Street by Lower Fitzwilliam Street. As you cross it, you'll see No. 29 on the right-hand corner. It has been restored in the style of a late eighteenth-century aristocratic town house and is open to the public. It is well worth a visit if you have the time.

Walk down one side of Upper Mount Street, around the church and back up the far side to rejoin Merrion Square. Upper Mount Street is one of the most pleasing and coherent streets in the city. The Irish-American writer Jimmy Breslin once pointed out that since it then contained the head offices of the country's two biggest political parties, as well as being the occasional haunt of prostitutes at night, people on the street got on real well since everyone was basically in the same line of business. Mount Street Crescent, embracing the church, gives on to another pleasant stretch of the Grand Canal — a happy diversion for those with extra time in hand.

Back on Merrion Square, turn right and walk along the east side with the façade of the National Maternity Hospital ahead. The 'Oxen of the Sun' episode of *Ulysses* is set here. Turn left at the hospital and continue along the north side of the square. Number 1 at the far end, now the American College, was the home of the eminent surgeon Sir William Wilde and his spirited wife Lady Jane who wrote patriotic verse for a paper called the *The Nation* under the pseudonym 'Speranza', something that a lady of her social standing was not supposed to do. Their son, the divine Oscar, grew up in this house. His memorial, a splendidly louche piece of statuary by Danny Osborne, stands (or rather reclines) across the street just within the limits of the park.

The park itself is worth a visit, if only for the perspective that it gives on the houses you have just walked past. Otherwise, it is conventionally municipal with neat flower beds and other manifestations of civic order.

The west side of Merrion Square, which we now rejoin, is dominated by Leinster Lawn (already mentioned) and the **National Gallery of Ireland**. Opened in 1864, the building was designed by Francis Fowke. At the entrance, there is a statue of George Bernard Shaw by Paul Troubetzkoy. Shaw

Merrion Square South with view of Pepper Cannister Church

left one-third of his estate to the gallery as a gesture of gratitude for the many hours of pleasure and instruction which he received here as an indigent youth. It was an important part of his self-education. Next time you hear some canting politician tell you that galleries and museums should always charge an admission fee because people don't appreciate things that are free, remember Shaw.

The gallery has a distinguished collection and is well worth whatever time you have to spare on it. It is particularly strong on seventeenth-century Dutch, French and Italian schools, with the most notable recent acquisition being Caravaggio's *The Taking of Christ*.

When you leave the gallery, turn left towards the corner of Merrion Square and Clare Street. Turn left again into Clare Street, passing Greene's quaint old bookshop, and continuing into South Leinster Street. The railings of Trinity College, enclosing College Park, are on the opposite side. Take the first major left-hand turn, into Kildare Street. The corner building, by Deane and Woodward, was the original home of the Kildare Street Club but is now occupied by the Alliance Française. The Royal College of Physicians is a little farther up on the left, a modest building. Opposite the opening into Molesworth Street stands Leinster House, originally built as the town house of the Duke of Leinster in the 1740s. It is now the home of the Irish parliament.

At the time the house was built, fashion still resided on the north side of the city. When friends protested to the Duke (actually he was only an earl at this stage; they didn't duke him until later) that he was building on the wrong side of town, he replied that wherever he was was the right side and that fashion would follow him. Arrogant little milord, but he was spot on – and the rise of the south side, together with the development of all the Georgian splendours we have just been touring, dates from that single decision. He was the leading nobleman in Ireland, and they followed him like sheep.

The matched buildings on either side as you face Leinster House are the National Library (left) and the main section of the National Museum (right). They date from the 1880s. The museum is, of course, open to the public and contains a fantastic collection of ancient Celtic and pre-Celtic artefacts, many of them of world importance. The Tara Brooch, the Cross of Cong and the Broighter hoard are just a few of the many items in this wonderful collection. The museum is simply not to be missed: it is a must-see, even if you only have a day to spare in the city.

Walk down **Molesworth Street,** laid out originally in 1727 but redeveloped progressively following the building of Leinster House. The street is dominated by the Masonic Hall built in 1865. The Freemasons were once quite influential in Dublin life (although believed to be vastly more so in the fevered imaginings of non-Masons). The building itself is worth a visit; it is handsomely ornamented and contains a small museum which is open to the public. Across the street, Buswell's is one of the city's favourite hotels. It was, until a few years ago, pleasingly singular and eccentric but it has been homogenised latterly. Which is a pity because, while it needed a facelift, it has been turned from a place with a real personality into just another comfortable hotel.

Some of the city's oldest Georgian houses are on Molesworth Street. At the end of the street, turn left onto Dawson Street. St Ann's Church faces down South Anne Street opposite, linking back to Grafton Street. It was built in 1720 to the design of Isaac Wills, with the present façade added by Deane and Woodward in 1868. Wolfe Tone was married here and the composer Michael Balfe was baptised in St Ann's. The musical connection has been sustained: the church is, in addition to being a place of worship, a popular concert venue.

Number 19 is the Royal Irish Academy, a scholarly institution which has played an important part in Irish intellectual life since its foundation in 1785. Among other pursuits, it is engaged on a vast multi-volume history of Ireland: the first volume appeared in 1976 and the series is still incomplete. A six-volume *Dictionary of Irish Biography* is well advanced, with the first volume due in 2004.

Next to the Academy is the splendid Mansion House, wherein resides the Lord Mayor. This worthy is elected annually by the City Council from among its membership. The position is entirely honorific. Although Dublin needs an executive mayor, along the lines of French or American cities, it won't get one. We prefer to follow the ineffective and inefficient English system of local government. So the Lord Mayor gets to wear a cape and a funny hat for a year and to open things and to make speeches (God help us) and stuff. The Mansion House was originally built as a private residence for Mr Joshua Dawson, the developer for whom the street is named, but never occupied by him. The Corporation bought it in 1715 and its present appearance is the result of many Victorian additions, including the fine entrance and the external plastering.

Cross to the other side of Dawson Street and walk back in the direction you have come. Pass the end of South Anne Street and go to the next side street on the left. This is Duke Street. Named for the 2nd Duke of Grafton, who was Viceroy of Ireland when it was laid out in the eighteenth century. On the left, at the Grafton Street end, is Davy Byrne's 'moral pub' where Mr Bloom famously lunched on a Gorgonzola sandwich and a glass of Burgundy on 16 June 1904.

Which brings us back to Grafton Street itself and the end of Day 1.

Temple Bar • Central Bank • Civic Offices • Christ Church Cathedral • St Patrick's Cathedral • Marsh's Library • Guinness Storehouse St Catherine's Church • Meath Street • Francis Street • Tailor's Hall • Brazen Head • Dublin Castle • Chester Beatty Library • City Hall

Day 2

Temple Bar and
the Old City

Day 2 Teaser

John Minot built it in 1370 and it is still there. What is it?

Temple Bar

Temple Bar is bounded by Dame Street, Westmoreland Street, Aston and Wellington Quays and Parliament Street. It is, therefore, quite a small area. Twenty years ago, it was just a dingy collection of neglected side streets. Three things made it.

First, most of it was owned by the national transportation company, which planned to turn the area into a vast national transportation centre. Second, this *folie de grandeur* never happened but it meant that the whole area was in public ownership and could be redeveloped as a unity. This is exactly what was done. A redevelopment company, armed with a brief to turn the area into a bohemian quarter, took the site over from the transport people. Third, and quite independent of all this, the area got its landmark, thumbprint building when the **Central Bank** of Ireland built its new headquarters on Dame Street.

No matter where you are in Temple Bar, this fine, brooding monster towers over you. It is the work of Sam Stephenson, one of the best Dublin architects of the last forty years. His view that in architecture 'apologetic self-effacement should be left to public lavatories, VD clinics and the other necessary minutiae of society' is well borne out here. There were endless rows over the Central Bank: the building's height exceeded that allowed in the planning permission by almost ten metres; opinion was divided between nervous conservationists who thought the building was a brutally intrusive behemoth and a minority who thought it the most exciting thing put up in the city in the twentieth century. A lot of people said: 'nice building, wrong location'.

Well, all that now seems like battles long ago. It is a good building in the right place, not perhaps as fine a structure as some of the more extravagant claims made for it would suggest, but a tremendous presence none the less. Of course, when it was finished in 1978 no one had any idea that Temple Bar was going to happen in its shadow. But it did.

You'll hear things about Temple Bar. It's phoney; it's all contrived; there are too many pubs with too many customers barfing on the pavement after closing time; the arts presence is an add-on, not integral to the area. And so on. This is all rubbish. Some of it is true (especially the pub bit) but it completely misses the point. Temple Bar saved the city. It gave Dublin a sense of the possible. This was a city in which almost nothing of quality had been built for decades. The abominations of the 1960s were fresh in the memory: it was as if Dublin was good for destroying the

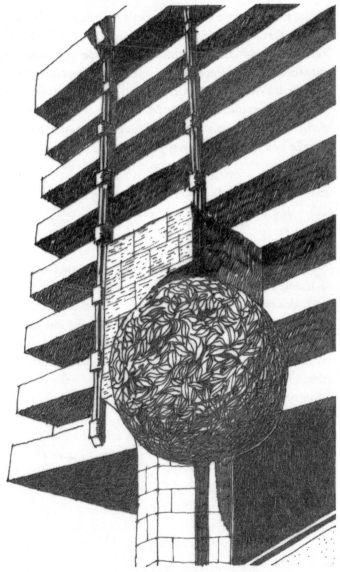

Central Bank, Dame Street

best of the old while building nothing of quality in its place. Temple Bar reversed all that. New public spaces were created; old buildings, long derelict, were restored and transformed. Apartments were built. Theatres and galleries appeared. People came. They walked around; they ate; they hung out; they looked happy. Most of all, they were young. In the late 1980s, Dublin was suddenly a young city and Temple Bar was *the* young space.

Because it is a small area, you can enter it at any point, wander around and not get lost. The simplest way to get a fix on Temple Bar is to walk west along Fleet Street from the corner of Westmoreland Street. After a few hundred metres you reach the open area called Temple Bar Square. On your right, Merchant's Arch links to the quays and the Halfpenny Bridge; on your left, Crown Alley runs down from the back of the Central Bank. The Bad Ass Café in Crown Alley is a good place for kids and the last place in the city where you can still see old-fashioned overhead vacuum tubes used to zip the cash to the cashier. The corner of Crown Alley and Cope Street is a riot of psychedelic paint, as emblematic of the city in its way as Georgian fanlights. Walk along Cope Street, duck right into Fownes Street and immediately left into Cecilia Street (the dominant building on your right was the original site of the UCD Medical School). Put your head into Claddagh records before crossing Temple Lane on the left diagonal and entering Curved Street. This is the city's newest street: it simply did not exist before the redevelopment. It leads to Eustace Street (the Temple Bar Information Centre is at No. 18) which you cross and enter the lovely, shallow-stepped passage that leads to Meeting House Square.

This too is all new, and a terrific space it is. The dominant building, on the east side, is the Ark — the first theatre in Europe built specifically for children. It has a reversible stage so that in fine weather shows can be performed in the open air. There is a good food market held in Meeting House Square every Saturday morning, a compulsory port of call for the *vrai bourgeois* of Dublin.

Essex Street East, which is a continuation of Temple Bar itself, brings you to the back door of the Clarence Hotel. This stands on the site of the old custom house, the one that was replaced by the present beauty downriver, James Gandon's masterpiece (pp 81–3). The Octagon Bar has long been a Dublin landmark. The hotel owes its current cachet principally to the fact that it is owned by the band U2. They have put serious money into refurbishing the place without destroying its ambience. At the corner of Essex Street and Parliament Street stands the Porter House, one of the first of Dublin's micro-brewery pubs. They brew their own beers on the premises and I can vouch for their Oyster Stout (and indeed for all their excellent beers). As Guinness chases the youth market with ice-cold stout — a crime against nature — the micro-breweries look like the last, best hope of discerning drinkers.

There is little point in holding your hand and directing you to every nook and cranny in Temple Bar. Half the fun of the place is just wandering around and discovering things for yourself. Once you realise that, on the Temple Bar-Essex Street East axis, you are always just a block from Dame Street on one side and the quays on the other, you can't go wrong.

PERSONAL FAVOURITE PLACES IN TEMPLE BAR

Gallery of Photography

Arthouse

Porter House

Merchant's Arch

The Ark

Irish Film Centre

Civic Offices

Leave Temple Bar proper by crossing Parliament Street and walking along Essex Street West. The Viking Adventure Centre is on your right. It is a multimedia re-creation of what the original Viking settlement was like over a thousand years ago. You travel on a virtual longship, arriving at the little settlement of Dyflin as the real Vikings might have done in their day. The exhibit also recreates the sights, sounds and — very important, this — the smells of the Viking town. There is a well-preserved longship and a good Viking museum, operated in conjunction with the National Museum.

Continue along Essex Street West. A brief diversion into Fishamble Street on your left brings you to the site where once stood the Charitable Musical Society's Music Hall, long since demolished, in which the very first performance of Handel's *Messiah* was given on 13 April 1742. Six years later, his *Judas Maccabaeus* also received its first performance on this site.

Cross Fishamble Street and slip into the Civic Offices complex, a pleasant urban space. The Civic Offices were the source of what was perhaps the greatest of all Dublin's recent architectural *causes celèbres*. It all started in the late 1970s, when the Dublin Corporation decided to develop the site as an office block for its clerical functionaries. Snag: this was the very oldest part of the city, right beneath Christ Church Cathedral, and archaeologists were frantically excavating what were the remains of the original Viking settlement. There was a huge public furore, which was settled eventually by an agreement which allowed more time (but not as much as the archaeologists would have wished) for excavation, following which building began.

The architect was Sam Stephenson. He built the first half of the scheme, the two blocks higher up the hill. Everyone hated them. They were immediately dubbed 'the bunkers' for reasons that are still self-evident to this day. The outcry against them was so great that work was suspended on the rest of the site and the twin bunkers stood there on the hill, right next door to Christ Church, like a pair of unloved orphan twins. The rest of the site, running down to the river, was derelict — awaiting the completion of Stephenson's plan. But opinion hardened inexorably against this, resulting in a stand-off. It was only resolved by replacing Stephenson's plan for the lower section with the elegant, horizontal building designed by Scott, Tallon & Walker which now occupies the site. Externally, it is best viewed from the far side of the river. Internally, it has a fine atrium which is well worth a visit.

All in all, the saga of the Civic Offices has resulted in a

workable compromise. The net outcome has been a pleasing building at a sensitive location on the quays.

Christ Church

Turn up Winetavern Street, heading for Christ Church which is connected to its Synod House by a bridge which you walk under. The entrance to the cathedral is on Christchurch Place, just to the left beyond the bridge.

This hill is the site of the original Viking settlement. The cathedral itself is a Viking foundation, making it unusual among cathedrals in northern Europe, nearly all of which are Norman in origin. A wooden structure, it dated from 1038; elements of the Viking church remain in the crypt. The Normans rebuilt it in stone in the late twelfth century but the cathedral remained in a neglected state from the sixteenth to the late nineteenth century. It was rebuilt and restored in the 1870s with funds provided by the distiller Henry Roe. The building you see today is largely the result of this restoration; it might more properly be called a reconstruction, since very little of the original medieval church survived Roe's improvements.

The crypt is the most interesting part of the cathedral and is well worth a visit. The tomb of Strongbow (Richard de Clare, the leading Norman *conquistador* of the twelfth century) is also a popular attraction, although its historical authenticity is very dubious. Strongbow was originally buried here but his tomb was damaged when a wall and part of the roof collapsed in 1562; what you see here is a replacement effigy of later date.

Christ Church

The bridge connecting the cathedral proper to the Synod House was built as part of Roe's redevelopment. The Synod Hall is the site of 'Dublinia', a multimedia exhibition which re-creates the social life of medieval Dublin from the arrival of the Normans in the 1170s until the Reformation in the 1540s.

St Patrick's Cathedral

From Christ Church, it is a short walk along Nicholas Street to St Patrick's Cathedral. This is the national cathedral of the Church of Ireland (as distinct from Christ Church which is the diocesan cathedral for the united dioceses of Dublin and Glendalough). It is often wondered at why such an overwhelmingly Catholic city should have two Protestant cathedrals and no Catholic one (see St Mary's Pro-Cathedral, pp 105–6). The answer is simple: history. At the time of the Reformation, all the city's churches passed into the keeping of the state church — and there they stayed, even after the Church of Ireland was disestablished in 1869. Indeed, it is worth recalling that for at least two centuries after the Reformation the city had a Protestant majority.

St Patrick's dates from 1190, when Archbishop John Comyn built a stone church to replace an older wooden structure. It was believed that St Patrick had baptised pagans at a well on the site. The present building dates from the first half of the thirteenth century. The tower was added by Archbishop Minot in 1370 following a fire and the spire in 1739. Like many another church, it was badly knocked about by Cromwell in the seventeenth century (the Lord Protector used it as a stable). As with Christ Church, it was the subject of a major restoration in the nineteenth century.

Where Christ Church was restored with whiskey money, St Pat's was restored with beer. Its benefactor was Sir Benjamin Lee Guinness, who engaged Sir Thomas Drew to undertake the work. A statue of Guinness by John Henry Foley stands near the entrance.

The most celebrated memorial in St Patrick's is the grave of Jonathan Swift (1667-1745) who was dean of this cathedral from 1715 until his death. Although born in Dublin, he regarded his return here from London as a form of exile. He had been a close confidant of the Tory political leadership which was ousted on the death of Queen Anne. With his Whig rivals now in office, Swift was fobbed off with an appointment in what he considered a dismal provincial town, far removed from the elegance and influence of the artistic and political beau monde. He was right: early eighteenth-century Dublin was a backwater. Its days of Georgian splendour still lay in the future, after Swift's death.

Swift was, in the opinion of many, the greatest satirist in the English language. This deeply misanthropic and unhappy man did, none the less, gain the love of two remarkable women, Hester Johnson (Stella) and Esther Vanhomrigh (Vanessa). There is much controversy and ambiguity about Swift's relationships with these women: it is speculated that he did not fully reciprocate Vanessa's love, while it is possible that he was secretly married to Stella. One thing is sure: he and Stella lie side by side in death in St Patrick's. Nearby is a bust of Swift by Patrick Cunningham dating from 1775 and containing the Latin inscription which Swift wrote as his own epitaph, noting that he lies 'where savage indignation can no longer rend his heart'.

The choir is the best preserved part of the medieval cathedral. It includes the grave of Marshal Schomberg, the Williamite general who died at the Battle of the Boyne (1690). In the south transept, an old door with a rough hole cut in it is the source of one the English language's more useful cant phrases. In the 1490s, the earls of Kildare and Ormond had a furious row which resulted in Ormond taking refuge in this part of the cathedral behind the door. When a reconciliation was reached, a hole was cut in the door and Kildare reached in his hand in friendship, not knowing whether it would be clasped or cut off. He was thus the first person 'to chance his arm'.

St Patrick's is the finest church in the city and it carries the weight of Anglo-Irish history on its walls. The heraldic and regimental banners, the tombs and effigies (of which the Boyle memorial, erected by the great Earl of Cork, father of Boyle the physicist, is the biggest) and the memorial plaques mark its special place in the Irish past.

Marsh's Library

When you leave St Patrick's, go around the corner into St Patrick's Close to one of the city's hidden gems. Marsh's Library, established by Narcissus Marsh, Archbishop of Dublin, in 1707, is the oldest public library in the country. It still looks much as it did in the eighteenth century. It has a collection of over 25,000 titles, including some very rare books and incunabula.

When you leave Marsh's, you can return in the direction of Christ Church either by Patrick Street and Nicholas Street or — better again — by Bride Street and Werburgh Street. This brings you past St Werburgh's church which has a wonderful interior that quite belies the shabbiness of the exterior. Although normally locked, it is open for Divine Service every Sunday at 10 a.m. Across the street from St Werburgh's is a Dublin institution, Leo Burdock's fish and chip shop — reckoned by connoisseurs to be the city's finest.

OPTIONS IN THE LIBERTIES

The main part of this day's touring takes us straight to Dublin Castle, but for those with extra time in hand, here are some options in the Christ Church area. The area immediately to the west of Christ Church is known as the Liberties. The name originally referred to lands outside the city walls which were prone to attack from the nearby mountains. These lands were granted variously to the archbishops of Dublin and the Earl of Meath, on the basis that they would exercise palatinate jurisdiction (i.e. control of taxation and law and order in return for providing for the area's defence). The Liberties — the name stuck long after the area became part of the city proper — was traditionally one of the poorest corners of the city. It is still so.

The simplest itinerary is to go straight to the farthest point from Christ Church and then work our way back. That means a walk along High Street, Cornmarket and Thomas Street (all a single, continuous thoroughfare) until you come to Guinness' brewery.

If Dublin is synonymous with any single product, it is the black, bitter stout with the creamy head made here. At its best, it is one of the world's great beverage drinks. At its worst, it is awful — and the key is temperature. Guinness should be lightly chilled. The modern market, however, is for ice-cold beers. So Guinness has had to alter the brew to facilitate extra chilling. The result is a kind of black lager, assiduously pedalled by the company with an ice blue label announcing that the drink is 'extra cold'. Even when it is not chilled to extra cold levels, the changed brew seems — to my taste at least — thinner and less substantial than it was previously, with less of that lovely malty aftertaste that was a distinguishing feature of a good pint.

Still, all that said, when it is good it is outstanding. No more complaints. Compared to most of the world's commercial beers, this is still a princely drink. It all began in 1759 when Arthur Guinness, a young brewer from Celbridge, Co. Kildare, bought the brewery which stood on the original twenty-four acre site here from Mark Rainsford, for whom the nearby Rainsford Street is named. Over the main entrance to the brewery, you'll see the foundation date on one side of the gate and the current year painted on the other.

The **Guinness Storehouse** is the tourist heart of the brewery. Occupying a huge building originally constructed in 1904 and recently converted into a state-of-the-art visitor centre, it gives a complete overview of the history, brewing processes and advertising campaigns that have turned Guinness into one of the world's greatest brand names. It is all here: information on cooperage, various forms of transport and all the other arcana of the brewing trade. Spread over five floors of this brilliantly adapted building, the Guinness Storehouse is one of the best visitor attractions in the city. One of the first guests here following its opening in December 2000 was President Bill Clinton. The views from the bar on the seventh floor — where you can sample the product — are the best in Dublin.

Walk back along Thomas Street toward Christ Church. At the corner of Thomas Court, the building on your right is **St Catherine's Church**. This structure, dating from 1769, stands on a much older ecclesiastical site. For years, its neglected condition was a disgrace to the city but it has been beautifully restored by CORE, a Christian evangelical group. It is one of those renewal projects that really lifts the heart. The patriot, Robert Emmet ('the darlin' of Erin') was hanged across the street in 1803.

Just beyond the opening for **Meath Street**, the National College of Art and Design is on your left, occupying the former premises of Powers' distillers. Meath Street itself is worth a dander; it is the bustling shopping street of the Liberties. The side streets connecting it and **Francis Street** contain the Iveagh market, another example of Guinness philanthropy, being a fine late Victorian structure. Francis Street itself is the place to go hunting for antiques. There

Guinness Brewery

are bargains to be had here for discerning collectors.

Rejoin Thomas Street (actually Cornmarket at this point). The fine Victorian Gothic church on the far side is that of St John the Baptist and St Augustine, an Augustinian foundation designed by the younger Pugin. It is known universally in Dublin simply as John's Lane church.

Stay on the right-hand side of Cornmarket/High Street as you return towards Christ Church. Turn right in to Back Lane and on your left you will come to the **Tailor's Hall**. This is the last remaining trade guild hall in the city. It dates from 1707. In 1792, the patriot Theobald Wolfe Tone, secretary to a body known as the Catholic Committee, leased the Tailor's Hall for a convention which quickly acquired the nickname of 'the Back Lane parliament' The delegates to the committee had been elected in an orderly manner. In the eyes of the Protestant Ascendancy, the Back Lane parliament was a startling assertion of Catholic solidarity. They were right: it was one of the staging posts on the road that eventually led to the rebellion of 1798.

Tailor's Hall itself was saved in the 1960s by a civic-spirited group of citizens under the leadership of Desmond and the late Mariga Guinness. The state had — yet again — allowed an historic building to decay to the point that the Dublin Corporation (wouldn't you know it?) declared it in danger of collapsing.

Go back to High Street and cross to the far side (tricky business, this, so be careful). The large, solitary church with the classical front is St Audeon's Catholic church dating from 1846. Just behind it is the much older and more significant Protestant church of the same name. It stands on a very early Christian site associated with St Columcille and retains many of its original medieval features, although it has not entirely escaped from 'restoration'. The baptismal font is dated 1194 and the nave is early thirteenth century. Nearby, St Audeon's Arch is the only surviving gate from the medieval walled city. A small section of the city wall has been restored beside it.

It is a short walk back to Christ Church to rejoin the main itinerary. Before you do, you may want to wander down to the end of Bridge Street, almost on the river, to the **Brazen Head** — allegedly the oldest pub in the city, or at least the one most continuously present on the same site — for a libation. Even if you had one in the Storehouse, another one won't kill you now.

Dublin Castle

The rising ground above the Liffey was a natural site for a fortress. In medieval times it was protected on one side by the river itself and on two others by a curving tributary called the Poddle, long since built over. It now gives into the Liffey through an opening in the wall on Wood Quay. In *Ulysses*, Joyce noted that as the Lord Lieutenant of Ireland, Lord Dudley, was riding past in his carriage en route to an official engagement, 'from its sluice in Wood Quay wall under Tom Devan's office Poddle river hung out in fealty a tongue of liquid sewage'. At any rate, the two rivers — main stream and tributary — had the effect of making that part of the hill an easily defensible site. So it was here that King John decided, in the early thirteenth century, to built the principal royal fortification in the city. For over 700 years, the Castle was the epicentre of royal power in Ireland.

To get to the Castle, walk along Christchurch Place and Lord Edward Street. The Cork Hill entrance takes you into the Upper Castle Yard. This space is essentially that of the original fortress. In medieval and early modern times, it lurched between gradual decay and desultory restoration. None the less, it was never successfully attacked or besieged. The only significant attempt, by Silken Thomas, Lord Offaly, during the Kildare rebellion of 1534, was beaten off. It was not until the coming of peace in the eighteenth century that most of the present structure of the castle was put in place and it assumed a ceremonial as well as a defensive rule.

Of the medieval castle, only the Record Tower and parts of the Bermingham Tower remain. Even at that, the Record Tower was 'restored' by Francis Johnston in the nineteenth century. The State Apartments, on the south side of the Upper Yard, are the principal visitor attraction. They include the splendid St Patrick's Hall (1783), in which the presidents of Ireland are inaugurated.

The former Clock Tower building, together with a new exhibition building to which it is attached, is the new home of the **Chester Beatty Library**. Sir Alfred Chester Beatty (1875–1968) made a fortune in mining. He was a passionate and discriminating collector and he gradually built up the world's largest private collection of oriental manuscripts. He moved to Dublin and in 1953 he built a special library at his house in the suburb of Ballsbridge to house the collection. He bequeathed the entire collection to the Irish nation. It is this collection which has now been moved from Ballsbridge into the Castle, a much more suitable venue for these priceless treasures.

Here you can see Babylonian clay tablets, ancient papyri, Russian and Armenian texts and over 250 manuscript versions of the Qur'an. In all, the collection boasts almost 4,000 Turkish, Persian and Arabic manuscripts; Chinese and Japanese *objets d'art* including the silk Chogonka Scroll, a seventeenth-century Japanese masterpiece; and important early Christian manuscripts which make the library a major international resource for Biblical scholars. The Chester Beatty is a must see.

In the Lower Yard, the former Chapel Royal (1814) is also the work of Francis Johnston, working on this occasion not in the classical style which was his stock in trade but in the fashionable Gothick style of the day. Sadly, the Lower Yard is also defaced by a ghastly office building for the accommodation of bureaucrats.

City Hall

For a happier example of what the city can achieve, leave the Castle and go next door to the City Hall which stands on Cork Hill facing down Parliament Street towards Capel Street bridge. This was originally built by Thomas Cooley as the Royal Exchange in 1779. It has functioned as City Hall since 1852. Over many years, the original design was compromised by screens, partitions and other intrusive enclosures. But now a wonderful restoration has taken place, faithful to Cooley's original plans and an absolute revelation. A building that had been disregarded for years is suddenly and magically one of the sights of the city.

It features an exhibition entitled 'Dublin's City Hall: the story of the capital'. But the real story is the rediscovery of one of the city's very finest classical buildings. Here is a stellar example of what real restoration can achieve. Full marks to the often maligned Corporation for their enlightened sponsorship of this triumph.

Next door to the City Hall, on Dame Street, there is a silly little micro-park with three female figures who may represent the trades of Dublin or the Three Graces or the Three Stooges or something. They stand on large, flat circular disks which remind you of nothing so much as a sewage pumping station.

On which cranky note, we end Day 2.

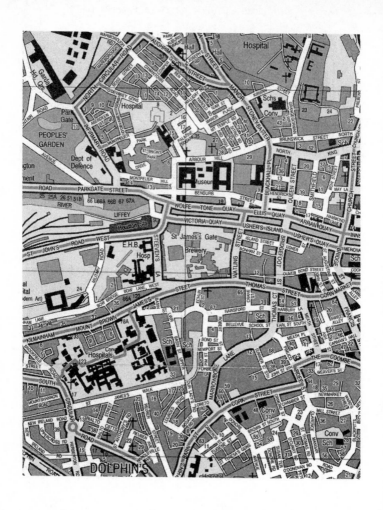

• South Quays • Heuston • Irish Museum of Modern Art •
Kilmainham • Phoenix Park • National Museum Collins Barracks •
Arbour Hill • Incorporated Law Society • North Quays • Smithfield
• St Michan's • Four Courts • Custom House • Irish Financial
Services Centre

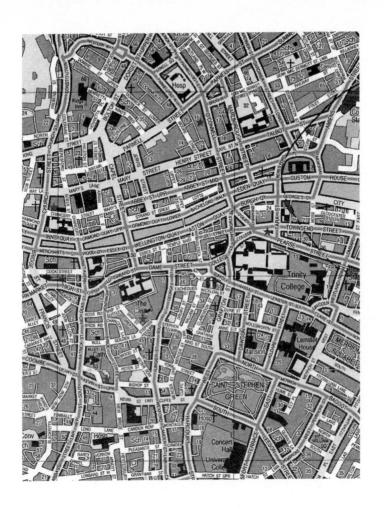

DAY 3

The Quays and the Park

Day 3 Teaser
It used to stand on the quays, but not any more.
What is it?

Lot of walking today. Start at the corner of Westmoreland Street and Aston Quay. You are going to walk the length of the **south quays** down to Heuston station. The Dublin quays are unremarkable for the most part. Their charm derives from the slightly shabby sense of unity in diversity. In places, as you'll see, that 'slightly shabby' becomes very shabby, but in general the quays are being renewed. Some of the newer buildings — especially some of the recent apartment blocks — are very pedestrian but at least they are in keeping with the traditional scale and elevation of the surrounding buildings. Only the Four Courts breaks the consensus: an undeniably great building, asserting itself massively over everything around it.

The first bridge you come to (but do not cross) is Wellington Bridge, although never, ever referred to as such. Not one Dubliner in a hundred would know it by this name. It is the Metal Bridge — or more usually the Halfpenny Bridge from the toll that was exacted in order to cross it from the time it was erected in 1816 until 1922. This elegant, single-span metal arch is one of the iconic

62

symbols of the city. It links Merchant's Arch and Liffey Street on the north side.

The next bridge is the city's newest. The Millennium Bridge, as the name suggests, was opened in 2000. Another elegant single span, it also links Temple Bar with the increasingly trendy north quays. It and the Halfpenny Bridge are the only pedestrian bridges across the Liffey. You soon pass the front of the Clarence Hotel and at the next bridge, named for the patriot Henry Grattan but always called Capel Street Bridge for the street that gives on to it from the north side, there is a remarkable piece of architectural confectionery on the far corner, at the end of Parliament Street. This is Sunlight Chambers, a gloriously Italianate dog's dinner. Built in the early twentieth century for a soap manufacturer, it caused conventional opinion at the time to foam like the soap itself. It was a hideous and unruly intrusion into the serenely classical city, they said. Well, yes, it is a bit naïve and vulgar but it is also great fun and we would not wish to be without it now. It has been cleaned recently and looks brand new.

Beyond Sunlight Chambers, on Essex Quay, there is an infill of new buildings which is one of the most satisfying recent developments in the city. The whole point is their stylish ordinariness. This is the outer reach of Temple Bar and the sense of style that is Temple Bar at its best is manifest here. These buildings are better seen from the north quays, so watch out for them on the return leg of today's trip.

Next is the turn for Fishamble Street and then we are on Wood Quay where we pass the Civic Offices. Past

O'Donovan Rossa Bridge — named for the Fenian Jeremiah O'Donovan Rossa, but always simply called Winetavern Street Bridge — and we are on Merchant's Quay. The Franciscan church known only as Adam and Eve's recalls the fact that during the penal era, when Catholicism was persecuted, a former church on this site was concealed behind a pub whose sign showed Adam and Eve in the garden. Joyceans will pause at this point, recalling the opening of *Finnegans Wake*: 'riverrun, past Eve and Adam's, from swerve of shore to bend of bay, brings us by a commodius vicus of recirculation back to Howth Castle and environs'.

The next bridge is unusual in that it is as often known by its official title, Fr Mathew Bridge, as by the colloquial Church Street Bridge. Fr Theobald Mathew (1790–1856) was the most celebrated Irish temperance campaigner of the nineteenth century. In the 1830s and '40s, the years immediately before the Great Famine, he weaned tens of thousands of Irish people — many of them the poorest of the poor in an impoverished country — off alcohol. Taking the pledge became a commonplace. It was an important step on the way to a more orderly, civic society and the campaign had the active support of the leaders of Irish nationalism, including the great Daniel O'Connell himself. 'Ireland sober is Ireland free', was the catchcry. Fr Mathew's campaign echoed similar movements in other modernising societies. In England, for example, under the influence of the Evangelical revival the Hogarthian nightmare of Gin Lane was replaced by the dreary virtue of Samuel Smiles. Fr Mathew's campaign was a rough Irish parallel.

Usher's Quay is next, with its eccentric petrol station. After Queen Street Bridge (officially named for the revolutionary republican Liam Mellowes) we come to Usher's Island. This was, unsurprisingly, once a small island formed by the Liffey and a number of tributaries that converged around this point. By the time the Liffey quays were completed in the mid nineteenth century, it had been filled in but retained the old name. No. 15 is the house in which Joyce's greatest short story, 'The Dead' was set. It was the home of the Misses Julia and Kate Morkan, the fictional analogues of two of Joyce's aunts: 'after the death of their brother Pat, they had left the house in Stoney Batter and taken Mary Jane, their only niece, to live with them in the dark, gaunt house on Usher's Island, the upper part of which they had rented from Mr Fulham, the corn-factor on the ground floor.' At the time of writing, it is sadly neglected. Happily, a public-spirited Joycean has bought the building and intends to restore it.

Victoria Quay completes the journey to Heuston Station. It was built in the nineteenth century to provide access to the new railway station and to give Guinness, whose premises had by then spilt down the hill from St James's Gate, access to the river.

Heuston Station

Heuston is named for Sean Heuston, a young officer in the Irish Volunteers who occupied the Mendicity Institution on Usher's Island in the Easter Rising of 1916. With less than twenty colleagues, he held the building from Easter Monday until midday on the Wednesday before overwhelming numbers of crown troops forced his surrender. He and his men inflicted over a hundred casualties on the British. Heuston was executed along with other leading rebels after the Rising was crushed. He had been a clerk in the Great Southern & Western Railway headquarters in the nearby station.

In those days, it was called Kingsbridge. Indeed, this name survived until 1966 when all the Dublin railway stations were renamed for rebel leaders as part of the golden anniversary commemoration of the Rising.

The Great Southern & Western Railway was founded in 1844. It was the largest of the regional railways which were later amalgamated into a single national system. The GS&WR thought of itself very much as the premier line. Whatever about that, it certainly built itself the finest terminus in the country. Designed by the London architect Sancton Wood, it presents a fine classical face to the quays. When it was built, all this area was open fields. It took years to complete – the railway itself was functional long before the station was finished. It was (and still is) the gateway to Cork and Limerick. The arms of these two cities, along with those of Dublin, are reproduced in stone castings on the parapet.

Royal Hospital/IMMA

When the GS&WR was established, its approach to Dublin crossed land belonging to the nearby Royal Hospital. This is one of the most interesting buildings in the city, both in its own right and because it houses the Irish Museum of Modern Art.

The principal interest in the Royal Hospital arises from the fact that it is the only monumental building put up in the city in the seventeenth century. Indeed, it was really the first such building in the city since medieval times. The series of wars and disturbances that afflicted Ireland as a whole from the 1530s to the start of the eighteenth century had seen to that.

The Royal Hospital was founded as an old soldiers' home. Designed by Sir William Robinson, the surveyor-general of Ireland, it opened in 1684. The model was Les Invalides in Paris, as it was for Chelsea Hospital in London which opened two years later. The site had previously been the priory of the Knights Hospitallers which did not survive the dissolution of the monasteries. It is a pleasing building, with a fairly obvious French influence. The chapel is particularly fine.

The Irish Museum of Modern Art opened here in 1991. It houses the leading collection of Irish and international contemporary art in the country.

Kilmainham Jail

Not far from the Royal Hospital, at Inchicore Road, Kilmainham Jail stands broodingly. From 1795 until its closure in 1924, it was the city's principal prison. It is not beautiful but it is, even by Irish standards, exceptionally historical. Most of all, it is sacred soil: it was here, in the stonebreakers' yard, that most of the leaders of the 1916 Rising were executed. This fact alone ensured that the empty jail has been faithfully preserved. You can visit the cells, see the fatal yard and learn much about Ireland's troubled past. Many leaders of the 1798 rising were imprisoned here, as was Robert Emmet a few years later. In the 1880s, the great nationalist leader Charles Stewart Parnell was here. The last person to be released from Kilmainham before it closed for good was none other than Eamon de Valera: as the political leader of those nationalists who rejected the Anglo-Irish Treaty of 1922 he was considered a threat to the fledgling Irish state. Not until the civil war — fought between pro-Treaty and anti-Treaty forces — was won by the new government was it thought safe to release him. Eight years later Dev was running the country.

Opposite Kilmainham, at the South Circular Road entrance to the Royal Hospital, stands the curious Richmond Tower. It used to stand at the junction of Watling Street and Usher's Island. But the development of Victoria Quay following the coming of the railway made it a traffic obstacle and it was moved up here in 1846. The architect was Francis Johnston.

Kilmainham is the farthest point out of town on today's itinerary. At this point, the simplest thing to do is to get any bus headed for the city centre and make the short journey down to Parkgate. This brings you to the head of the north quays, on the far side of the river from Heuston station.

OPTION: PHOENIX PARK

As the name Parkgate suggests, the main entrance to the Phoenix Park is here. At 709 ha / 1,752 acres, it is one of the largest enclosed parks in the world completely within a city boundary. All the same, this is a bit of false claim because the Park is not central to Dublin in the way that Central Park is to New York, or Hyde Park or the Bois de Boulogne are to London and Paris. That said, it is a fabulous resource and one which is much underused by Dubliners themselves.

The best way to see it is to walk it, which is why I'm treating it as an optional feature. You simply won't have time to do this and complete the regular itinerary, unless you are a masochist or an Olympic wannabe.

I'm not going to suggest a whole walking tour because it would be silly. You'll see why the minute you start to stroll in the Park. The simplest thing is to point out the principal places of interest. You can choose to discover as few or as many of them as your heart desires and your feet allow.

First, however, some background. The name Phoenix is thought to be a corruption of the Irish words *fionn uisce* (pron. *fee*yun *ish*ka), meaning clear water and referring to a spring near what is now the centre of the Park. It was first enclosed in 1662 as a vice-regal deer park. There are deer in the Park to this day. It was Lord Chesterfield, the worldly cynic who was a friend of such writers as Gay, Arbuthnot and Pope, who laid the basis of the modern public park. Chesterfield was lord lieutenant of Ireland in 1745-6. The main road through the park, from Parkgate to Castleknock, is named for him (another one of those facts not known to all Dubliners).

WELLINGTON MONUMENT

Dublin's most obvious phallic symbol commemorates Arthur Wellesley, 1st Duke of Wellington, probably the greatest commander in the history of the British army. He was born in Mornington House, Merrion Street — now incorporated into the Merrion Hotel — in 1769. He did care to be described as Irish, famously remarking that a cat born in a stable is not a horse. The decision to erect the monument was taken almost two years before Waterloo, a sign of the prodigious reputation the duke had achieved. He had made his name in India and consolidated it in the Iberian Peninsula from 1809 onward. Beginning with his back to the sea in Portugal, he gradually drove the French out of that country, then out of Spain and finally occupied Toulouse in 1814. At Waterloo the following year he secured the final victory over Napoleon.

The foundation stone for the Monument was laid by Lord Whitworth , the lord lieutenant of Ireland, in 1817 but it did not assume its final appearance until the bronze panels commemorating Wellington's military victories were put in place in 1861. They were cast from cannon captured in the Peninsular War. At 60 metres tall, the Wellington Monument is the biggest obelisk in Europe.

ZOO

The Zoological Gardens date back to 1830. Dublin Zoo is the second oldest in the world; only London Zoo, in Regent's Park, is older. It is a well-loved Dublin institution, and rightly so: it even has a well-known ballad written about it, which is fame of a sort. Quite apart from the animals, who are fascinating in themselves, the grounds are lovely. A stroll in the zoo is a very pleasant way to pass an hour or so.

ARAS AN UACHTARAIN

Or, in English, the President's House. It was originally the viceregal lodge, the official residence of the lord lieutenant (or viceroy) of Ireland. Built in the 1750s by Nathaniel Clements as a hunting lodge but elaborated by Francis Johnston in 1816, who provided the portico and other dignifying features. Although closed to the public, it can be clearly seen from the road. Nearby, the official residence of the United States' ambassador to Ireland was formerly that of the chief secretary of Ireland. He was the British cabinet minister who carried political responsibility for the country; this distinguished him from the viceroy, who represented the crown, and whose rôle was mainly ceremonial. Abutting the ambassador's side wall, on the edge of the Fifteen Acres, stands the large white steel cross which commemorates the visit of Pope John Paul II to Ireland in 1979; he celebrated Mass here before a congregation of over a million. It is the only time in history that Ireland has had a papal visit. That said, the cross is crass: it is too big and assertive and triumphalist.

THE PHOENIX COLUMN

This stands in the centre of the park astride Chesterfield Avenue. This was its original position but for many years it stood to one side, near the gates to Aras an Uachtarain, having been moved there to accommodate a motor racing circuit in the Park. It was an obstruction to the racing cars.

Happily motor racing — a brainless activity if ever there was one — did not flourish in the Park which was therefore rescued for quietness. In 1990, the column was restored to its proper position. The Phoenix Column is misleading, inasmuch as it perpetuates the myth that the Park draws its name from the mythical bird which arises from its own ashes. However, it is a pleasing deception. The spring for which the Park is really named is not far from here.

ST MARY'S HOSPITAL

Between the papal cross and St Mary's Hospital lies the Fifteen Acres, a wide open expanse of parkland. Parts of it are laid out as football pitches. It is here that you are most likely to see the Phoenix Park deer herd. Why this area is called Fifteen Acres when it is clearly much bigger than that, I don't know. St Mary's Hospital was originally the Royal Hibernian Military School, built to the design of Thomas Cooley in 1766. It provided an education for the orphans of soldiers, and continued to serve this purpose until the end of British rule in 1922.

MAGAZINE FORT

Now a ruin, the Magazine Fort stands on Thomas' Hill near the southeastern corner of the Park. It was built in 1734 and inspired Swift's lines: 'Lo, here's a proof of Irish sense. / Here Irish wit is seen. / When nothing's left that worth defence, / They build a magazine.' In 'A Painful Case', one of the finest stories in *Dubliners*, Mr Duffy retreats here after learning of the death in a railway accident of Mrs Emily Sinico, the unhappily married woman whose offer of love he had spurned. At the base of the wall, in the darkness, he notices some courting couples and knows that they resent his presence, while he is repelled by 'their venal and furtive loves'. The fort continued to serve a military purpose after the British left and was used as an arms depot by the Irish army for some years. On Christmas Eve 1939, when security was not exactly over-zealous, the fort was raided by an IRA contingent. So successful were they that in not much more than an hour they got away with thirteen lorry-loads of ammunition — more than a million rounds. They had pretty well cleared out the Irish army's entire reserve supply.

THE FURRY GLEN

This is at the western end of the Park, near the Knockmaroon Gate. It is a deep wooded area with a small reedy lake. It was once a popular place for courting couples, being remote and quiet. In one of the city's more scabrous ballads, dating from the 1880s, we are told that W.E. 'Buckshot' Forster, the unpopular chief secretary, spent some time there:

You've heard of Buckshot Forster
The dirty ould imposter
He took a mot [girl] and lost her
In the Furry Glen.

He then put on his bowler
And he buttoned up his trousers
And he whistled for a growler [horse cab]
And he said, 'My man! Take me up to Monto...,

Monto being Dublin shorthand for the brothel area behind
O'Connell Street.

ORDNANCE SURVEY

The nearby premises of the Ordnance Survey of Ireland
was previously the Mountjoy Barracks, reflecting the
military origins of the OS. It was originally built as a
private house by Luke Gardiner, founder of the dynasty
that developed the Georgian north side (see p. 87). The
Survey dates from 1838 and among other things it made a
profound mark on Irish life by anglicising place names of
Irish-language origin in the course of its early mappings.
Thus *baile* (a town, pron. bol-ya) became Bally-, the most
common of all Irish place name prefixes. The semantic
and cultural confusion thus caused is the theme of Brian
Friel's play *Translations*.

National Museum at Collins' Barracks

The main itinerary resumes where we left it, at Parkgate.
Walk along Parkgate Street, a rather dingy thoroughfare
but one that contains one of the city's best-loved pubs,
Ryan's. This is a perfect late Victorian bar, in more or less
pristine condition (see 'Ten Essential Pubs'). If you find
yourself in this area around the middle of the day, you can
lunch either in the bar itself or in the more formal
restaurant upstairs.

The route to the National Museum's second collection at
Collins' Barracks is either along Wolfe Tone Quay and
Sarsfield Quay followed by a left turn into Liffey Street

West or directly along Benburb Street. The slightly longer route has the advantage of taking you past a green area with a memorial at the far end. This is Croppies' Acre, a burial ground in which were interred (or flung) the bodies of rebels from the 1798 rising. They were called Croppies because of their habit of wearing their hair close-cropped in the French revolutionary fashion.

Collins' Barracks is named for the eponymous Michael, hero of the Irish revolution. Formerly, it had been the Royal Barracks. It was built by Thomas Burgh, the same architect who designed the Old Library in Trinity. The parade ground is the largest in Ireland. The Irish army took it over from the British. They in turn vacated it in the mid 1990s and the museum took it over. The collection concentrates on the decorative arts. There are excellent collections of textiles, ceramics, furniture, silver, glassware and weaponry: don't miss the gauntlets worn by King William at the Battle of the Boyne in 1690.

A short distance away, at **Arbour Hill**, is the main memorial to the executed leaders of the 1916 rising who are buried here. When you leave, walk down the ever-narrower Arbour Hill until you reach the corner of Stoneybatter. It was on this corner that the twelfth chapter — episode if you want to be posh — of *Ulysses* begins with the unnamed narrator passing the time of day with old Troy of the Dublin Metropolitan Police. A careless chimney sweep went by, nearly driving his brushes into the narrator's eye. As he turned to remonstrate with him, 'who should I see dodging along Stony Batter only Joe Hynes.' The pair of them tag along together to Barney Kiernan's pub in Little Britain Street, where the rest of the action occurs.

Stoneybatter and Arbour Hill are part of an area called Oxmantown (named for the Ostmen, or men of the east, or Vikings who settled there after the Norman incursion). It was the earliest settlement on the north bank of the river.

Stoneybatter and its northerly continuation, Manor Street, are raffishly shabby and very pleasant. Worth a five-minute detour. The main route is, however, right at the end of Arbour Hill along Blackhall Place with the intention of rejoining the north quays. On your right, you will pass the premises of the **Incorporated Law Society**, the self-regulatory body for the solicitors' profession. It was formerly King's Hospital, not a hospital in fact but a school. Better known simply as the Bluecoat School, it was founded in 1699. This building was designed by Thomas Ivory and erected in 1773. It was to have had a much more dramatic tower, which would have given a vertical balance to the composition, but this was never built. The present apologetic tower is a poor substitute.

Smithfield

Rejoin the river at Ellis Quay, pass Queen Street Bridge and take the first turn on the left. This brings you into Smithfield. There are dramatic plans afoot to transform this former fair ground into a vital urban space. The north side is already much restored but at the time of writing, it will be another two or three years before the south side, with its access to Queen Street and Blackhall Street, looking towards the Bluecoat School, will be redeveloped.

The north side has seen the development of a hotel, apartments, restaurants and shops. It is dominated by the Chimney, an old distillery chimney which has been converted into a viewing tower and platform. It is the second-tallest structure in the city and the helpful guides take you up in the newly installed outside lift. It's a no-no if you suffer from vertigo; otherwise it is recommended.

Likewise Ceol (Irish for music), which is the Irish Traditional Music Centre which introduces you to the riches of the Irish folk music tradition using state-of-the-art audiovisual technology. The 180° widescreen auditorium is particularly impressive.

This area was dominated by Jameson's distillery, one of dozens of such enterprises in nineteenth-century Dublin. The name has survived because it is now the brand name by which Irish whiskey is sold internationally. In the old days, its product was known in Dublin simply as JJ&S, after the label on the bottle standing for John Jameson & Son. When Joyce feared that he might not be able to finish *Finnegans Wake*, he thought to ask James Stephens (with whom he reputedly shared a birthday, something of significance to the superstitious Joyce) to finish it for him. The idea was that the book would have been titled *JJ&S*, for James Joyce and Stephens.

The old Jameson distillery in nearby Bow Street has now been turned into an excellent museum called the Irish Whiskey Corner. It caters for visitors in a wide variety of languages, including Japanese. Distilling is universal in northerly latitudes and Irish whiskey traditionally enjoyed a good international reputation until elbowed aside by commercial blended Scotches (horrible drinks, for the most part, unlike their peerless single malts) in the early twentieth century. The fightback is now on. A visit to the Irish Whiskey Corner gives one an insight into a product that goes very far back in Irish history: you can also sample the product. The Jameson distillery itself was founded in 1780.

St Michan's

Around the corner in Church Street, St Michan's is named for an eleventh-century Viking martyr-bishop. It has been much knocked about and restored over the years, not least in the brief civil war of 1922-3, when there was a rebel garrison in the nearby Four Courts. For centuries, it was the only church on the north side of the Liffey. Edmund Burke is among the celebrated people associated with the church: he was baptised here in 1729. What makes the church famous, however, is the vaults. The magnesium limestone of which they are constructed has the property of absorbing moisture. In the dry air, corpses are preserved. Some of these mummified remains are in a remarkable state of preservation and are a major tourist attraction. One sniffy writer declared that they 'do not merit their vulgar exploitation', which makes them sound very worthwhile.

Four Courts

The Four Courts on Inns Quay is the most imposing building along the river front. It is the centre of the Irish legal system and was the one of the last monumental classical buildings to be completed in the city. Designed by

Four Courts

James Gandon, construction began in 1786 and lasted sixteen years. The original four courts, from which the building takes its name, were those of the King's Bench, Exchequer, Chancery and Common Pleas.

Although the building cannot simply be wandered through as if it were a museum (no obvious jokes, thank you!), it is worth stepping into through the main entrance to admire the splendid round hall. The courts themselves, of course, permit public access subject to the availability of space. The Irish legal system is based on English Common Law, although the effect of European Union law, whose roots are in the very different Roman tradition, is growing by the year. Legal practice differs in one important respect from England. There, barristers (that is, lawyers who have rights of audience before a court as distinct from solicitors who basically prepare the office work) are not organised in different chambers. Instead, there is a single Law Library in the Four Courts to which barristers have exclusive access. It has been the tradition of the Library that any member who is consulted by a colleague on a point of law must immediately suspend what he is at in order to help with the query. On other matters, however, the English influence persists, not least in the question of dress. Barristers still wear wigs and gowns, something that upsets some people because it allegedly makes the barristers appear remote and intimidating. Personally, I think that a bully in a suit is no better than a bully in a gown. And the wigs and gowns do look exotic.

The best view of the Four Courts is the one you had earlier, walking along the south quays and looking across the river.

On the north side, up close, you appreciate the sheer monumentality of the building. Much of what you see here was rebuilt in 1932, ten years after this wonderful building was destroyed in the Civil War. The war was fought on the question of whether the new Irish government had extracted enough concessions from the departing British. The government claimed that it had, the opposition that it had betrayed the republican ideals of the independence movement. Republican irregulars occupied the Four Courts and other public buildings in the city. In a surreal re-run of 1916, government troops shelled them out of it, except that this time it was an Irish government doing the shelling. The republicans surrendered after two days. However, they had maliciously booby-trapped the Strong Room of the Public Record Office housed in the building. They knew what they were doing, putting at risk the single most significant collection of historical records in the country. Over a dozen booby-trap bombs were successfully dismantled by government troops before one — better concealed than the others — exploded. It blew the room to smithereens and with it priceless, irreplaceable records, some of them dating back to the twelfth century. The super-patriots blew up their own country's history, or at least the means of telling it. It was the worst and most wicked act of cultural vandalism in twentieth-century Ireland.

The Custom House

The Custom House is Gandon's other great river-front building and, in the view of many, his masterpiece. To get there from the Four Courts, it is a simple stroll along the north quays. On Ormond Quay Upper, you pass the Ormond Hotel where the 'Sirens' episode of *Ulysses* was set, although I doubt that Simon Dedalus would recognise the place today. Cross the end of O'Connell Street and walk along Eden Quay. Before you are the two vilest structures in the city, Liberty Hall and the Loopline Bridge. Liberty Hall was stuck up in the mid 1960s, a bad time for architecture in most places and a disaster for it in poor mimetic, provincial Dublin. It should be pulled down. Likewise the Loopline Bridge which dates from 1891. This unsightly monster connects Pearse Station in Westland Row to Connolly on the north side: it is the only city-centre railway crossing on the river. There is talk from time to time of replacing it with something sleek and modern but so far it has remained at the level of talk.

Both Liberty Hall and the bridge featured in the 1916 rising. The Irish Citizen Army — a trade union militia — was based in the old Liberty Hall on this site. It was from there that it and the Irish Volunteers mobilised before marching around to O'Connell Street to occupy the GPO. Later the British sailed an armed fisheries protection vessel called the *Helga* up river to a point opposite the Custom House. The idea was for her to shell rebel positions, starting with Liberty Hall. The British believed it to be a rebel nest, whereas it was empty except for an unfortunate caretaker: the real rebels were in the GPO. *Helga* fired off a shell which clattered into the Loopline Bridge with a boom that was heard all over the city. On the principle that it is hard to kill a bad thing, the bridge survived. The gunners then adjusted their sights, figured out their angles a bit better and vaulted the next shell neatly over the bridge to flatten the original Liberty Hall.

The Custom House was completed in 1791 after a series of disputes so vicious that the architect, Gandon, had taken to walking around Dublin with a sword for his own protection. Like the Four Courts, it is best seen from the far side of the river. It was built for a commercial purpose and it still houses the offices of a government department. This seems a pity. A building with such a noble exterior is effectively closed to the public and discharges no vital civic function. The bureaucrats could push their pens in any office block in Dublin. It would be a fine challenge for the city to find a rôle for the interior of the Custom House worthy of its wonderful exterior.

The Custom House is built of Portland stone. Like the Four Courts, it suffered in the Troubles of 1919-23. During the War of Independence (1919-21) it was attacked by the IRA and fired. It was rebuilt but the cupola was done not in Portland but in the much less attractive Ardbrackan stone. At the back of the Custom House, facing Gardiner Street, stands a memorial sculpture to the Dublin Brigade of the IRA by the Breton sculptor Yann Renard-Goulet.

Nearby, on the curve of Memorial Road stands Busaras (bus house to you), the central bus station. Designed by Michael Scott, it was the last word in modernism when it opened in 1953. It was the first large building of any consequence erected in the city centre for decades. Although it has not weathered well, it remains a pleasing building and one with much potential. That potential might be served best by re-locating the bus station elsewhere rather than at one of the most tangled junctions in the city.

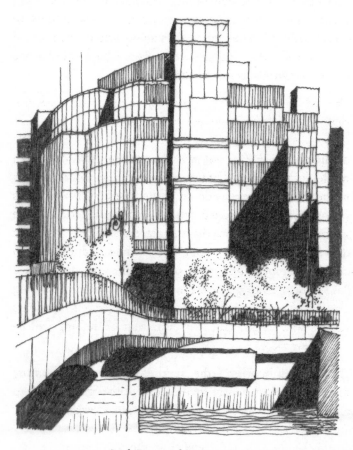

Irish Financial Services Centre

IFSC

Just east of the Custom House, the International Financial Services Centre dates from the late 1980s and presents some of the most attractive modern architecture in the city. A formerly decayed site on the edge of the docks, it was revived by a government-sponsored scheme which gave tax breaks and other incentives to financial institutions to locate here. It was denounced by many when first mooted but has been a resounding success, as much a symbol of the revival of Dublin as Temple Bar.

The IFSC is well worth a wander. There is much more to it than the attractive river front buildings. There are apartments, open spaces, restaurants and pubs in the complex. The IFSC is not just attractive in itself, it is also a model for the renewal of the entire riverfront on both sides of the Liffey all the way down to the East Link Bridge. This process is more advanced on the north quays than on the south, but the plans are there on both banks and it is to be hoped that they will be brought to fruition. Just down from the IFSC, a hugely ambitious plan for the redevelopment of the Spencer Dock area is on hold at the time of writing because of objections from local residents and others to its density and height. But it is clear that something will be built on the site.

Dublin is rediscovering the river. The city is re-orientating towards the Liffey after generations in which the flight to the suburbs effectively rejected the river and with it the city centre itself.

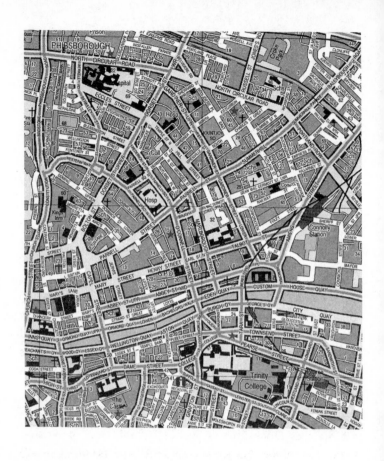

• O'Connell St. • Statues • Rotunda • Parnell Square • Garden of Rembrance • Hugh Lane Gallery • Writers' Museum • James Joyce Centre • Nth Gt George's St. • Mountjoy Square • Gate Theatre • Pro-Cathedral • Abbey Theatre • [Blessington St. basin] • [Henrietta St.] • [King's Inns]

Day 4

North Inner City

Day 4 Teaser

Where is the only square in Dublin?

When Dublin was founded by the Vikings, it was on the rising ground south of the river around Christ Church. Apart from Oxmantown directly opposite the walled city, medieval Dublin did not cross the river. In the early eighteenth century, therefore, when the city began to break out of its medieval redoubt, it pushed in every direction: east downstream, symbolised by the eventual removal of the Custom House from Wellington Quay to its present location and southeast towards St Stephen's Green and the Georgian squares. But most of all, it pushed north. Classical Dublin first developed on the north side of the river. And that is where we are concentrating today.

If the Fizwilliams built the south side, the Gardiners built the north side. The founder of the dynasty was Luke Gardiner, a banker. In 1714, he bought a holding just north of the river from Henry Moore, Earl of Drogheda. He had begun to lay out streets in this area. Thus we had Henry Street, Moore Street, Earl Street, Of Street and Drogheda Lane (later Drogheda Street and then Sackville Street and now O'Connell Street). The Gardiners added to their holdings over the next three generations and it was they who developed much of the north side east of Capel Street.

The second Luke Gardiner, son of the first, was ennobled as Viscount Mountjoy and died at the Battle of New Ross during the 1798 rising while leading the Dublin Militia against the rebels. The family also became Earls of Blessington. All three names — Gardiner, Mountjoy and Blessington — feature prominently in the estates they laid out.

O'Connell Street

The main street of the capital is the only one to have any pretensions to be a genuine boulevard. When first laid out by the Earl of Drogheda and more particularly by Luke Gardiner, it was a classically perfect and unified Georgian street. Time, decay, revolution and neglect have changed all that. It still has charm along with the tackiness and its sheer scale is impressive.

Let us start at O'Connell Bridge, at the southern end of the street. It was first built in 1795 to a design by Gandon. It was considerably narrower than Sackville Street. The present structure was designed by one of the half-forgotten geniuses of Victorian Dublin, Bindon Blood Stoney, chief engineer of the Dublin Port & Docks Board. It opened in 1880 under its new name, O'Connell Bridge.

Immediately in front of it, dominating the southern end of the street, stands John Henry Foley's O'Connell Monument. Daniel O'Connell (1775–1847) was the effective father of modern Irish nationalism and one of the most remarkable men in nineteenth-century Europe. Indeed, he was a figure of European importance and had a reputation as such — for he was both a Catholic and a liberal, a combination otherwise thought impossible in the conditions of post-French Revolutionary Europe. He mobilised the Irish poor in a successful campaign for Catholic Emancipation, i.e. the removal of legal barriers to Catholic advancement which had existed since Reformation times. His subsequent campaign for the Repeal of the Act of Union and the restoration of a Dublin parliament was less successful but, in one form or another it became the irreducible demand of all Irish nationalists thereafter. He was the first European political leader to mobilise mass opinion; in so doing, he invented populist democratic politics. He was Europe's Andrew Jackson.

Foley's wonderfully coherent memorial is a fitting testimonial to an extraordinary force of nature. The Liberator — as he was known to his contemporaries — stands aloft with four angels attendant representing Courage, Fidelity, Eloquence and Patriotism. You can clearly see bullet holes in the angels which are a legacy of the 1916 Rising, while poor Dan is permanently shampooed in seagull shit.

O'Connell Street itself suffered from the decay that affected the entire north side following the Union of 1800 and the flight of fashion to the south side. The erection of Nelson Pillar in 1808, commemorating the British naval commander killed at the Battle of Trafalgar — it was blown up by the IRA in 1966 just to show how damned anti-British we could be — and the building of the imposing GPO in 1814 permanently altered the appearance of the street. The Easter Rising of 1916 wrought immense destruction and the Civil War of 1922–3 compounded it. The street was rebuilt in the 1920s by the then city architect, Horace Tennyson O'Rourke. And a remarkably fine job he made of it. His was not the Georgian street *revividus*. But it was a sensitive reconstruction which acknowledged the proportions of the past. Up to the 1960s, O'Connell Street was still self-consciously the principal street of the city — not the most fashionable, but the grandest. It was a well-bred but indigent *grande dame*.

Then came two different varieties of poison: the IRA and property developers. The former blew up Nelson Pillar, the very umbilicus of the city, and the latter did what they did everywhere in that dismal decade for architecture: replaced the dignified with the trite.

So now, as we walk north along the west side of O'Connell Street, we start with an unbroken terrace of fast-food joints all the way from the bridge to the corner of Abbey Street. There are other such joints further up the street, not to mention 'amusement arcades' where witless, deluded poor fools play video games and one-armed bandits. The Corporation has a plan for the regeneration of the street and everyone who cares for Dublin wishes it luck.

Between Abbey Street and Henry Street, Eason's Bookshop is a Dublin institution. The original Eason was manager of W.H. Smith's branch in Dublin. Smith became a Conservative MP and was appointed to Disraeli's government in 1874. As an office holder, he had to divest himself of his business interests (those were the days). He placed his English business in a trust but sold his Irish branch to his manager Eason.

O'Connell Bridge and Street

Beyond Eason's, the whole street is dominated by the colonnades of the General Post Office. Built to the design of Francis Johnston, it was famously the headquarters garrison of the Irish Volunteers during the 1916 Rising. The Rising is recalled most graphically by Oliver Shepherd's statue of the dying Cuchullain — an ancient Celtic hero of legend — which stands in the main hall. Happily, the GPO has not been converted to some naff 'heritage' purpose but continues to sell stamps and perform all the other post office functions.

The west side of the street from the GPO up to Parnell Street contains a few pleasing buildings — including the very last original Georgian house on the street at No. 42 — as well as some dreck. In *Ulysses*, Mr Bloom thought to himself that this was a dead part of the street and it remains the least vibrant to this day. Bloom wondered why, if it had something to do with sun or wind. He did not know and neither do I.

The east side of O'Connell Street is dominated by two buildings. Between Abbey Street and Earl Street, Clery's department store is one of the city's landmarks. People still meet under Clery's clock. Farther up the street, the splendid Gresham Hotel is still one of the best in the city. Architecturally both buildings are very fine, although very different, and each was a part of Horace Tennyson O'Rourke's restoration.

O'CONNELL STREET STATUES

The statues and monuments that occupy the middle of O'Connell Street, going north from the O'Connell Monument, are:

Daniel O'Connell (1775–1847), patriot, by John Henry Foley with winged figures by Thomas Brock

William Smith O'Brien (1803–64), patriot, prominent Repealer and leader of the doomed affray at Ballingarry, Co. Tipperary, later inflated into the 1848 rising, by Sir John Farrell

Sir John Gray (1816–75), proprietor of the *Freeman's Journal*, the leading nationalist newspaper, and promotor of the Vartry water supply system which provided pure piped drinking water for the city for the first time, by Sir Thomas Farrell

James Larkin (1876–1947), labour leader, syndicalist and founder of the Irish Transport & General Workers' Union (now SIPTU). He led the union during the Lockout of 1913, the most famous labour dispute in Irish history. This statue, by Oisin Kelly, is based on a celebrated photograph of Larkin taken almost on this spot.

Father Theobald Mathew (1790–1856), temperance campaigner, attributed to 'Miss Redmond'

The Millennium Fountain, representing Anna Livia (the River Liffey), presented to the city by the Smurfit family and universally referred to as The Floozie in the Jacuzzi. It is the work of Sean Mulcahy and Eamon O'Doherty. The millennium in question was the (completely bogus) celebration of the city's millennium in 1988, a mere forty-seven years late. The name Anna Livia is of Norman provenance, being a transliteration of the Irish *Amhain na Life* (pron. Ow an na Liffe), meaning the River Liffey.

The Parnell Monument, commemorating Charles Stewart Parnell (1846–91), the greatest nationalist leader of the late nineteenth century, who established home rule as a central ambition for Ireland and a central problem for Britain, by Augustus St Gaudens

Rotunda

The Roto, as it is known to generations of Dublin women, dates from 1755 and was the first maternity hospital in Ireland. It stands at the top of O'Connell Street on Parnell Street. It was founded by Bartholemew Mosse in 1755. The architect was Richard Castle, a German who did much work in Dublin in the mid-eighteenth century. This is a fine public building but in order to maintain it Mosse — who was something of an entrepreneur as well as a midwife — built additional rooms in which entertainments could be staged to help defray the hospital's costs. (One of these is now the Gate Theatre.) Likewise he opened the Rotunda Gardens to the public at a price and they quickly became the centre of fashionable society in the years when this part of the city was still *tres chic*.

The really sensational part of the Rotunda is the chapel, a Baroque extravaganza with plasterwork by Barthelemy Cramillion. It is the only place of worship in Dublin executed in a genuinely Baroque manner. Dublin, with its low church traditions, preferred chilly classicism to the exuberant fripperies of the Baroque. The Rotunda chapel is a glorious exception to the rule. Access is confined to worshippers during services.

Parnell Square

Reflecting the relative decline of the north side, Parnell Square (formerly Rutland Square) has little of the stately self-possession of Merrion or Fitzwilliam Squares. Its immediate hinterland, particularly along Parnell Street, is hardly a help. Begun in the middle of the eighteenth century, by the end of the century it was still very grand. The central gardens were gradually built over as the Rotunda Hospital needed to expand: these buildings are strikingly insensitive to their surroundings. The rest of the site is now occupied by the Garden of Remembrance.

The north side of the square was always the grandest and in the peculiarly abiding way of such things, it still is. The dominant building is Charlemont House, the town house of James Caulfield, Earl of Charlemont, dilettante and Whig grandee. He was the leader of the fashionable *beau monde* in late eighteenth-century Dublin and in addition to this house he also commissioned Sir William Chambers to design the exquisite Casino at Marino (p. 122). Charlemont House became the Municipal Gallery of Modern Art in 1932 which was later renamed for Hugh Lane, its greatest benefactor.

Hugh Lane Gallery

Hugh Lane was a nephew of Augusta, Lady Gregory, one of the prime movers of the Irish literary and cultural revival of the late nineteenth and early twentieth centuries. He established a very successful art dealership in London as a young man, showing great flair and taste. He was also a collector in his own right. In 1914 he became director of the National Gallery of Ireland. He generously offered his own collection, mainly comprising French impressionists and other work still regarded as *avant garde* by contemporary opinion, to the city of Dublin, if it would built a permanent gallery worthy of it. No less a person than Sir Edward Lutyens proposed a dramatic building on a new bridge over the Liffey.

The wretched philistine Corporators rejected the proposal on grounds of cost — the cry of the pinched provincial everywhere — and Lane withdrew the offer, gifting the pictures to the National Gallery in London instead. He then changed his mind and added an unsigned codicil to his will reverting the pictures to Dublin without conditions. None of this would have mattered much had he lived — he was only forty — but he went down with the *Lusitania* when returning from New York. There followed a dispute between the National Gallery in London which had the letter of the law on its side and Dublin which had the spirit of the law on its. Finally, there was a judgement of Solomon. The collection would be split between the two cities on a rotating basis.

So what you see in the Hugh Lane at any given time is half the Lane bequest plus the other pictures in the collection.

These include works by such Irish artists as Mainie Jellett, Mary Swanzy, Jack Yeats and Sean Scully and by an international variety of painters ranging from Millais and Burne-Jones to Monet, Rouault and Bonnard. The stained glass of the Irish master Harry Clarke is also a feature, in particular the stunning *Eve of St Agnes*.

The Hugh Lane has recently announced the receipt of a stunning gift, the complete studio of Francis Bacon as it stood at his death. It will be brought from London and faithfully reconstructed in Dublin. Bacon was born in Baggot Street and spent his early years in County Kildare. An exhibition of his work in the Hugh Lane in 2000 was one of the most successful in the city for many years. The Gallery hopes to develop a Francis Bacon archive which will become a major international scholarly resource.

Dublin Writers' Museum

Just along from the Hugh Lane, at Nos. 18–19 Parnell Square, is the Dublin Writers' Museum. The collection comprises letters, journals, portraits and other memorabilia associated with the many famous writers that Dublin has produced over the centuries. In a city so famous for its contributions to literature, it is surprising that a museum such as this was not opened until as late as 1991. Still, it is here now, housed in a really well restored Georgian mansion — it is worth going in just to look at the house — and including a very good café which is ideal for a light lunch.

Across the road, in all that remains of what were once the Rotunda Gardens, is the **Garden of Remembrance**. It commemorates the Rising of 1916 and was laid out in

1966, on the golden anniversary of that seismic event. The statue is by Oisin Kelly and represents The Children of Lir, an ancient Irish legend of three children who were turned into swans and condemned to live for 900 years. The spell was finally broken by St Patrick, who restored them to humanity and baptised them before they died. The choice of this legend, together with the cruciform design of the Garden itself, is testimony to the completely unconscious union of nationality and religion in 1966. Times change.

Before we continue, we can consider a detour at this point for those with time in hand.

OPTION: NORTH SIDE EXTRAS

At the corner of Parnell Square, turn left into North Frederick Street, cross the major intersection with Dorset Street and carry on into **Blessington Street**. Blessington Street bends to the right becoming Berkeley Street; ignore the bend and go straight on to the dead end that leads to one of the city's more charming secrets, Blessington Street Basin. Blessington Street, as the name suggests, was part of the Gardiner estate. The basin is all that is left of a terminus of the Royal Canal. An extension ran from the main canal down to this point. The Royal Canal was the less successful of Dublin's two canals. The Grand was finished before it and had more chance to recoup its development capital before the railways revolutionised everything. The Royal had not. When the extension was no longer needed, it was filled in and turned into a perfectly undistinguished linear park. But this quiet spot was salvaged and is there to enjoy.

Hugh Lane Gallery

You now have a choice. When you return to Blessington Street you may, if you are a Joycean with a strong stomach, cut down Nelson Street and into Eccles Street. Number 7, the most famous address in modern literature, the home of Leopold and Molly Bloom in *Ulysses*, is obliterated. Not by bombs or age but by a private hospital built in the sort of red brick that looks all right in an unambitious suburb and looks awful here. But then anything other than the original house would look awful here. The only consolation is that it probably would not happen now. The city has moved on too much for that, I hope...

Turn right at the junction of Eccles Street into Dorset Street, noting the fine church of St George across the way in Hardwicke Place. Designed by the ubiquitous Francis Johnston (who lived up the way at 64 Eccles Street) it was modelled on St Martin in the Fields in Trafalgar Square. Dorset Street soon rejoins the corner of Blessington Street, where non-Joyceans will already have made their way. Walk along poor, ruined Dorset Street Upper until it gives into Bolton Street and you come to **Henrietta Street** on your right. In the 1720s, this was it: the most fashionable street in the city. Indeed right through the eighteenth century, it was the best address in Dublin. It takes some imagination to reconstruct this area as it was in the heyday of the Gardiner estate but the sheer size of these houses in Henrietta Street is some help. They are absolutely enormous, much grander than anything put up in any of the Georgian squares.

Henrietta Street leads to the back of the **King's Inns**, the governing body of Irish barristers. The full title is The

Benchers of the Honorable Society of the King's Inns. This is the last of James Gandon's great Dublin buildings. Started in 1795, it was not finished until 1817. Gandon's pupil Henry Aaron Baker also worked on it, and the inevitable Francis Johnston put in his oar as well. There is no public entrance from this Henrietta Street side. The front of the King's Inns, where there is limited access, faces Constitution Hill and the disused Broadstone railway station: it is best seen from that side.

Around Mountjoy Square

From the corner of Parnell Square, we head across North Frederick Street and into Denmark Street. Looking back, we can admire the Abbey Presbyterian Church known to all Dubliners simply as Findlater's Church after the wealthy grocer who endowed it.

A short walk along Denmark Street brings us to **North Great George's Street** on the right. This street is a beacon of hope for the entire north inner city. Here is an area of great historical and architectural value where much has been long neglected and decayed. But North Great George's Street has been renewing itself for over twenty years. Enterprising and civic-minded citizens have bought houses and restored them as living spaces. The whole street has an air of confidence so noticeably absent nearby.

The James Joyce Centre is at number 35. It celebrates the life and work of the Master, organises readings and lectures, and will be of interest to everyone with any curiosity about the city's past. No city ever had a more detailed chronicler than Dublin had in Joyce.

And so back to the top of North Great George's Street. Facing you is Belvedere House, an eighteenth-century town house now part of Belvedere College, a Jesuit secondary school where Joyce was a pupil. The hell-fire sermon in the third chapter of *A Portrait of the Artist as a Young Man* was preached here. Turn right and continue into Gardiner Place before arriving at Mountjoy Square.

This was the *pièce de resistance* of the Gardiner estate. In many respects, it is the most satisfying of all the Georgian squares and for a very simple reason: it is the only one of them that is actually a mathematical square! That said, it is obviously neglected, although not as badly as it used to be. There is a long way to go before it is ever restored to its former state. We live in hope.

Looming away in the middle distance are the huge stands of Croke Park, headquarters of the Gaelic Athletic Association. The GAA, one of the most potent and enduring bodies in Ireland, organises the sports of Gaelic football (the biggest spectator sport in Ireland), hurling (don't miss it if you get a chance), camogie (women's hurling) and handball. It has built, largely out of its own resources, a world-class stadium for its games.

Gate Theatre

Retrace your steps to the corner of Parnell Square and turn left along the east side of the square, going downhill towards O'Connell Street. The old Rotunda Gardens are behind the railings on the right-hand side. Beyond them is the Gate Theatre, housed in what was originally the supper room of the New Assembly Rooms (1786), part of the commercial extension to the Rotunda Hospital complex mentioned earlier.

The Gate was founded in 1928 to complement the older Abbey. The Abbey was the national theatre, dedicated to the work of Irish playwrights. The Gate aimed to bring European theatre to Dublin. It was a heroic undertaking, for Dublin was not as self-consciously European then as it is now. In the 1920s, independence was still a novelty and all the emphasis was on what made Ireland different, unique, apart from other places. Europe was far away. Commercial air travel was still a decade away — farther for the mass of people — and the cost and inconvenience of travel kept most people at home.

The theatre's founders were Hilton Edwards and Micheál Mac Liammóir, both of them originally English. There was never much doubt about Hilton's origins but Mac Liammóir's ability to disguise and reinvent himself was astonishing. Throughout his life it was believed that he had been born in Cork — as he claimed — a story all too easy to believe as, among things, he spoke the most perfect, chiselled Irish you ever heard. It was only after his death that it was discovered that he had been born Alfred Willmore in London, had studied at the Slade and had worked as a young actor with Herbert Beerbohm Tree and Noel Coward. It was a mask that his hero, Oscar Wilde, would have applauded.

The Gate fulfilled its remit of bringing outstanding European theatre to Dublin faithfully for years, mainly thanks to the munificence of the Earl and Countess of Longford who made good the inevitable financial shortfalls. Serious theatre seldom pays: it never stood a chance in Dublin at the mid-century. Mac Liammóir's one-man show, *The Importance of Being Oscar*, a homage to Wilde, was a huge international success in his later career.

Since 1983, the theatre has been under the direction of Michael Colgan and has gone from strength to strength. It has toured internationally with acclaimed productions of O'Casey and Beckett — its *Waiting for Godot* is sensational — and has had hugely successful seasons of Pinter and Beckett in Dublin as well as a host of other fine productions.

Beside the Gate, facing down O'Connell Street, is the actual Rotunda building from which the whole complex — including the hospital itself — took its name. Built in 1764, it was designed by John Ensor — the architect of Merrion Square — as an assembly room. It is an historic space, shamefully abused and mistreated in the course of the twentieth century. The composer John Field — who first developed the nocturne, subsequently brought to perfection by Chopin, as a musical form — made his first public appearance here. Likewise Michael Kelly, the Irish tenor who was later a friend of Mozart and who sang in the first ever performance of *The Marriage of Figaro* in Vienna in 1786. The Volunteer Convention of 1783, an important contemporary event, took place here. Liszt played here. The Irish Volunteers — different from their eighteenth-century antecedents although consciously echoing their name — were founded here in 1913. Three years later, they tripped off the Easter Rising; a few years later they had mutated into the IRA of the War of Independence; a few years more and they had become the Irish army. So there is a lot of history here. It is sad to see this building, part of an outstanding complex in a part of the city that needs all the renewal it can get, not fully restored and dedicated to some public, civic purpose.

The Pro-Cathedral

Marlborough Street was part of the original Gardiner Estate, named for the Duke of Marlborough — founder of the Churchill dynasty — whose victories in the War of the Spanish Succession (1701–14) were the greatest feats of arms by a British general prior to Wellington. It runs parallel to O'Connell Street but was never as grand as it. When the whole area behind O'Connell Street declined, it declined with it. So it was here, in this nondescript and discreet side street, that the Catholics of Dublin thought it prudent to park away their principal church.

St Mary's Pro-Cathedral was built in 1815, at a time when official Dublin was still overwhelmingly Protestant and when assertive displays of Catholic renewal were not welcome. Thus the discreet location. It is a Pro-Cathedral in the sense that the Catholic Church did not recognise the legitimacy of the Reformation transfers of the real cathedrals — Christ Church and St Patrick's — to the Church of Ireland. They awaited the day when they could reclaim one or other or both. They are still waiting, and this is a subject on which there is now a blessed silence.

The architect was an amateur, John Sweetman. The Pro-Cathedral is his only known contribution to world architecture. It is designed in the style of a Greek temple, a contemporary vogue. The altar is by Peter Turnerelli, who, despite his name, was from Belfast of all improbable places. The glory of the 'Pro', however, is the Palestrina Choir. Originally endowed by Edward Martyn, a wealthy and pious minor *litterateur* who was involved with Yeats and Lady Gregory in the literary revival, it still sings magnificently every Sunday morning. If you like sacred music sung as it should be, *in situ* during a religious service, 11 o'clock Mass every Sunday morning in the Pro-Cathedral is for you.

The buildings opposite the Pro-Cathedral are the premises of the Department of Education. They include Tyrone House, a Richard Castle building dated 1740. It was the town house of Marcus Beresford, Earl of Tyrone, a member of a family hugely influential in eighteenth-century Ireland.

Abbey Theatre

Farther down Marlborough Street, at the junction of Abbey Street, stands the startlingly unsuccessful building that houses Ireland's national theatre. A piece of 1960s brutalism by the otherwise excellent Michael Scott, it has never established itself in the affection of the Dublin public. The entrance canopy and atrium on Marlborough Street are later additions.

The Abbey Theatre was founded by W.B. Yeats, Lady Gregory and others in 1904 in a premises on this site. Previously it had been the Mechanics' Institute, a working men's educational establishment. Yeats and Lady Gregory adapted it for their purpose and off it went on its wondrously erratic career. They were lucky. They had one playwright of genius, John Millington Synge, to hand and discovered another, Sean O'Casey, within twenty years. Synge's *The Playboy of the Western World* caused a riot in 1907 that established the theatre's reputation. Nationalists objected to the portrayal of Irish country people in the play and in particular to the use of the word 'shift' — this being an item of women's underclothing, a slip — by an Irish male. Likewise, when O'Casey's *The Plough and the Stars* caused a riot in 1926, it was because the tricolour — the national flag — was at one point carried into a public house wherein was Rosie Redmond, a prostitute.

These were triggers, not causes. The Abbey (indeed much of the literary revival) was largely a Protestant undertaking in a Catholic city. Yeats, Lady Gregory, Synge and O'Casey were all Protestants. Although Yeats was a radical nationalist and O'Casey a militant socialist, they were distanced from the ordinary *petit bourgeois* types who were the backbone of the nationalist movement by temperament and background. Yeats, of course, would have been an exotic in any milieu. The Abbey riots were a manifestation of these subtle social and sectarian tensions, not simply a one-dimensional stand-off between the forces of light and darkness.

But whatever they were, they made the theatre in its early

years. They gave Yeats a cause which informed his poetry and his public life thereafter. And to be fair to the rioters, they were, at least, upset by works of real theatrical power. Synge and O'Casey are acknowledged internationally as two of the more important anglophone playwrights of the century. And there is something to be said for a theatre that can move people so profoundly and for a culture that can be so moved. It is (or rather was) a fine old Parisian tradition as well.

Synge died young. O'Casey emigrated in 1928 after the rejection of *The Silver Tassie* by the Abbey. Lady Gregory died four years later. Yeats died in 1939. By then, the slide downhill was well on. In 1941 Ernest Blythe took over as general manager, a position he retained until 1967. If he failed to run the Abbey into the ground, it was not for want of trying. He was an ex-politician, Minister for Finance in the 1920s, and an enthusiast — some might say fanatic — for the revival of the Irish language. He was cultured but in an awfully narrow way. Combine this with a sure instinct for parsimony and a total lack of feel for what theatre could achieve as a public art form, and you had a disaster.

Then the theatre burned down. In 1951, the old Mechanics' Institute went up in smoke and the Abbey spent the next sixteen years operating out of the Queen's Theatre in Pearse Street, an old music hall. They returned to the sacred site in 1966 on completion of the present building, amid much joy.

Since then, fortunes have fluctuated. But at least the worst days are behind the theatre. In a sense, it is asked to perform an impossible rôle: to be a national theatre that constantly renews and deepens the traditional repertoire, while not neglecting international trends and discovering outstanding new Irish talent in each generation. The greatest living Abbey playwright is undoubtedly Brian Friel. From *Philadelphia, Here I Come* (1964) to *Translations* (1981) and the international smash-hit *Dancing at Lugnasa* (1990), he has produced a body of work that stands alone among his contemporaries.

The Peacock, a basement studio theatre for experimental work, is also part of the Abbey complex.

There has been talk of rebuilding the theatre yet again. There is dissatisfaction with the main auditorium as a theatrical space. It has even been suggested that the Abbey might move to the more congenial south side. This would be a disaster. The north inner city needs every civic and public institution it has plus lots more in addition. By all means rebuild — but rebuild here. And if not here, at least somewhere suitable north of the river.

From the Abbey, it is a short stroll to O'Connell Bridge where we began.

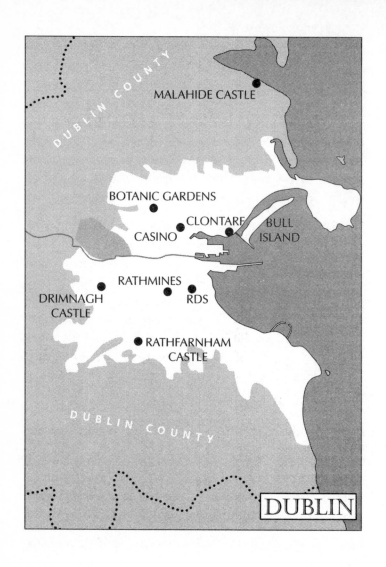

• RDS • Drimnagh Castle • Rathfarnham Castle • Rathmines and
Rathgar • Botanic Gardens • Casino • Bull Island • Malahide Castle

110

Day 5

Around the Suburbs

Day 5 Teaser

Here lie the bones of St Valentine. Eh?

Today's itinerary is necessarily a thing of bits and pieces. It cherry picks a number of worthwhile sights and activities in the suburbs. The map indicates their approximate location relative to the city centre but there is little point in giving detailed access instructions for each one. In all cases, except for Rathmines and Rathgar which is a walking route, I'll indicate bus routes: any bus route with an X is part of the Xpresso fixed-fare, exact-fare service. Hired car or taxis are the other options. There is nowhere in this day's route that is directly on the DART line: we're saving all that for tomorrow. We'll cover the southside in the morning and the north side in the afternoon.

RDS

Merrion Road, Ballsbridge, Dublin 4

Bus: 5, 7, 7A, 7X, 8 (all from Burgh Quay), 45 (from Eden Quay)

Nearest DART: Sandymount (5–10 mins)

The Royal Dublin Society is one of the true ornaments of Irish life. It was founded in 1731, having evolved out of the Dublin Philosophical Society of 1683. It received its royal charter in 1821, following the visit of King George IV. Its original purpose was the improvement of Irish agriculture as well as the general development of the arts and sciences. In 1815 it moved into Leinster House, which was its headquarters until 1924 when that building became the seat of the Irish parliament. Many of the great public institutions of Irish life were developed and matured under the aegis of the RDS: the National Library; the National Museum; the National College of Art and Design; the National Botanic Gardens; the Veterinary College and even the Zoo. Its historic connection with agriculture and the countryside generally is still maintained by its annual Spring and Horse Shows, the latter one of the highlights of the Dublin social season every August.

The RDS grounds, including the main show-jumping arena, are very attractive.

Nearby, the United States embassy is a pleasing circular building dating from the 1960s — an exception to the rule that that decade was a total disaster for architecture in Dublin. Beside the embassy, St Bartholomew's on Clyde Road is the only authentically High Church place of worship for those among the city's Church of Ireland community who welcome this option. The prevailing tendency in the Church of Ireland generally has been Low or evangelical, no doubt as an antidote to all that Catholicism around the place. But St Bart's is the place for Protestant bells and smells, if that's your fancy.

Drimnagh Castle

Long Mile Road, Dublin 12

Bus: 56A (from Eden Quay)

Way out in the southwestern suburbs, Drimnagh Castle is a well-restored medieval castle with formal gardens and a proper moat — not a dry moat, but one properly full of water. It is situated in the grounds of Drimnagh Castle Christian Brothers' School. The castle dates from the thirteenth century. It was built by the Barnwells, one of the great Hiberno-Norman families of the Pale. The Pale was the area around Dublin in which the direct influence of the English crown was strongest in the Middle Ages. The principal attraction is the Great Hall, one of the best restored in Ireland.

Rathfarnham Castle

Rathfarnham Road, Dublin 14

Bus: 15C (from College Street); 16, 16A, 16C (all from the Airport via the city centre with stops in O'Connell Street and South Great George's Street).

Rathfarnham Castle was built by Adam Loftus, Church of Ireland Archbishop of Dublin, in 1583. It occupies the site of an older twelfth-century structure. Interior decoration was added in the eighteenth century to the design of William Chambers. The castle was owned for many years by the Jesuits but is now in the care of the state.

Rathmines and Rathgar

No buses needed for this one. These are inner suburbs, just on the south side of the Grand Canal. They are typical of how the city developed after the heroic Georgian period. The Georgian style survived in Dublin until after 1850, partly because of its prestige, partly because of the city's conservatism and reluctance to embrace Victorian architectural fashions in vogue elsewhere. However, these suburbs show the mixture of styles very well, as the classical model gradually yields to suburban bourgeois red brick.

Indeed, a number of middle-class suburbs including these detached themselves municipally from the city in the nineteenth century. They established their own townships, complete with town halls and all the apparatus of local government. Why? To avoid the higher rates that were levied in the city. This further diminished the Corporation's revenue base, making the lot of an already desperately poor city even worse. People familiar with the American flight to the suburbs in the twentieth century, leaving ruinous and impoverished downtowns behind, will recognise the pattern. The independent townships were abolished in 1930 and reintegrated with the Corporation area.

Start at Portobello Bridge over the canal, at the point where South Richmond Street becomes Lower Rathmines Road. On the right, you pass the playing fields of St Mary's College, one of the city's leading boys' schools and a celebrated rugby nursery. On the opposite side, the great copper dome of the Church of Mary Immaculate, Refuge of Sinners dominates much of the south side of the city.

Rathfarnham Castle

This splendid structure dates from 1854; the architect was Patrick Byrne. Further along, on the left, is Observatory Lane. It is named for Thomas Grubb (1800-78), one of the greatest of Irish scientists. He was an engineer and optician and manufactured reflecting and refracting equipment for most of the leading astronomical observatories in Britain and Ireland. He was regarded as one of the world's leading experts in optics and Dublin thought so much about him that it renamed the little laneway where he lived and died in his honour. At the head of Observatory Lane, Leinster Cricket Club is one of the oldest sports clubs in the city, dating from 1852. The original charming red-brick pavilion survived until the last few years when the financial temptation to sell off the part of the ground on which it stood proved irresistible. Pity.

Back on Rathmines Road, you are now into the jumble of shops, pubs and other premises that give this area its charm. This is no longer merely a genteel suburb; it is student flatland as well, which lowers the tone nicely. Leinster Road, off to the right, is rather more sedate: it dates from 1855 and the Carnegie Library on the corner from 1913.

Opposite Leinster Road stands the very fine Rathmines Town Hall, an assertive red-brick statement of the old township's municipal independence dating from 1887. The architect was Thomas Drew.

Next on the left after the Town Hall is Castlewood Avenue, into which we turn. The artist Walter Osborne was born and lived all his life at number 5. You pass the very pleasing Belgrave Square on your right, cross the intersection at the top of Mountpleasant Avenue and find yourself on Charleston Road. There is a very fine example of architectural adaptation on your right, where a deconsecrated church has been successfully converted into offices. The route now takes you down into Ranelagh. The main village, not as raffish as Rathmines but pleasant none the less, is on your right but our route is left. Ranelagh Road goes under the broken bridge that used to carry the Harcourt Street railway line and rejoins the canal at Charlemont Street Bridge. As you draw ever nearer to the canal, you'll notice the Victorian styles yielding to the Georgian. An alternative, and very pleasant, Victorian alternative is to turn right into Dartmouth Road. This joins with Upper Leeson Street and allows you to regain the canal at Leeson Street bridge.

Mount Jerome Cemetery

Harold's Cross Road, Dublin 6

Bus: 16, 16A (see Rathfarnham Castle, above); 49, 49A (from Eden Quay)

The great southside necropolis, for all you graveyard fiends, is at the junction of Harold's Cross Road and Lower Kimmage Road. This is the last resting place of many Victorian luminaries. The cemetery is pleasingly laid out on a grid pattern around a central oval. It was traditionally a Protestant establishment, in contrast to the Catholic Prospect Cemetery on the north side in Glasnevin. Among the dearly departed interred here are Thomas Davis, the patriot; Sir William Wilde, the father of Oscar; and Edward Dowden, the literary critic and poetaster.

OPTION: OTHER INTERESTING ODDS AND ENDS

Portobello and the Grand Canal

The Portobello area at Charlemont Street Bridge is the best place to begin exploring the Grand Canal. If you followed the Rathmines and Rathgar route above, you will have found this already. Here was an old canal harbour and the fine classical building that dominates the view was an old hotel for travellers, rather like the railway hotels of a later age. From here you can walk along the canal east, passing Charlemont Street, Leeson Street and Baggot Street bridges. The canal is at its best on these stretches. You'll pass the Patrick Kavanagh memorial near Baggot Street Bridge. From there, go along Herbert Place, Warrington Place and Clanwilliam Place and so on to the interesting Waterways' Visitors Centre on Grand Canal Quay.

Irish Jewish Museum

One of the city's more poignant museums is to be found at 3 Walworth Road, just around the corner from Portobello Harbour. There you will see memorabilia of a community now sadly diminished in numbers and in danger of disappearing altogether from Irish life.

The Shaw Birthplace

George Bernard Shaw was born at 33 Synge Street, also around the corner from Portobello Harbour. It has been turned into a small museum to celebrate the life of this extraordinary force of nature: dramatist, critic, wit, socialist, vegetarian, windbag and, in his heyday, the most famous writer in the world. He is out of fashion at the moment, but there are cycles in literary fashion as in all else. The Shavian canon is too rich to be neglected indefinitely. He'll be back.

Whitefriar Street Church

Beneath the high altar of this Carmelite Church repose the remains of St Valentine, whose feast day on 14 February is a special day for lovers everywhere. The remains of the saint were sent from Rome to Dublin in 1836. The church also contains a statue of the Virgin dating from medieval times and recovered from the ruins of St Mary's Abbey (see below).

Baggot Street and Pembroke Road

From Fitzwilliam Street along Baggot Street towards the canal. You pass the massive head office of the Bank of Ireland, built in the style of Ludwig Mies van der Rohe. Dublin has accommodated itself to this assertive intrusion into the Georgian heartland, but there is no real public affection for the building. Once you cross the canal bridge you are in the pleasant bustle of Upper Baggot Street which then continues on as Pembroke Road. All in all, one of the most lively quarters in the city. The side roads off Pembroke Road, Raglan and Wellington Roads, are very fine examples of a late Georgian/Victorian *haut bourgeois* inner suburb.

St Mary's Abbey

Just off Capel Street, opposite the end of Upper Abbey Street, are the ruins of the chapter house of the Cistercian Abbey of St Mary, the greatest religious foundation in medieval Dublin. This was one of the finest buildings in the city and was often used as the meeting place for the councils that advised the English governors of Ireland. The abbey was suppressed at the dissolution of the monasteries in 1539.

The National Botanic Gardens

Botanic Road, Dublin 9

Bus: 13, 13A (both from Merrion Square with stops in Nassau Street and O'Connell Street); 19, 19A (both from Finglas to Inchicore via the city centre with stops at O'Connell Street and South Great George's Street).

Another one of those well-kept secrets. The Botanic Gardens are simply a delight — and not just in summer, although obviously at their very best then. They occupy almost 20 hectares beside the Tolka, a small river that bisects the north side of the city. Here are beautifully maintained walks, herbaceous borders, rock gardens and many varieties of trees uncommon in these latitudes. Most especially, there are the great curvilinear glasshouses, designed by Richard Turner and dating from 1843 to 1869, which have been magnificently restored in recent years. They support a large variety of tropical plants in appropriately steamy conditions. For green-fingered visitors, this is not to be missed. It has the added advantage of being relatively close to the city centre, so that if you are travelling out by taxi it is not a hugely expensive option. On one side, the Botanic Gardens abut onto Glasnevin Cemetery which is where we are bound next.

Prospect (Glasnevin) Cemetery

Finglas Road, Dublin 11

Bus 40, 40A, 40B, 40C (all from Parnell Street)

It would be easy to denominate it as the northside Mount

Jerome, but it is not. Glasnevin Cemetery (the official name, Prospect Cemetery, is hardly ever used) is the largest in the city. It began as a Catholic cemetery in 1832 at a time when Catholics were being denied burial rights in other cemeteries.

Daniel O'Connell was one of the chief instigators of the scheme. So it is fitting that he himself is buried here, in a vault beneath a grandiloquent replica round tower erected in 1869, twenty-two years after his death. A little distance away, on the other side of the mortuary chapel, is the most impressive grave in Ireland. A single boulder of Wicklow granite bears the simple legend: Parnell. These graves, of the two outstanding leaders of nineteenth-century Irish nationalism, summarise their characters. O'Connell was florid, theatrical, torrential, vulgar and immense. Parnell was remote, chilly, massively self-controlled, calculating, masterly.

In front of the mortuary chapel (1878) are mausoleums to various archbishops of Dublin. That for Cardinal McCabe (d. 1885) is particularly fine, being the work of the distinguished ecclesiastical architect George C. Ashlin. To the right of the entrance, there is a republican plot containing the graves of many leaders and men from the War of Independence, including Arthur Griffith and Michael Collins. Eamon de Valera is also buried in Glasnevin.

It was in this cemetery, on 16 June 1904, that the fictional Paddy Dignam was buried in *Ulysses*.

Casino

Off Malahide Road, near Griffith Avenue corner

Bus: 20B (from Eden Quay); 27 (from Talbot Street); 27B, 42, 43 (from Beresford Place); 42A, 42B (from Lower Abbey Street)

This is the most exquisitely perfect classical building in Dublin. The fact that it is in an unsympathetic location should not deter you. It is a truly beautiful thing, worth taking trouble over. Take any of the buses listed above and alight at the first stop after you pass the end of Griffith Avenue, which joins Malahide Road on your left.

When it was built, this was open country, gently rising ground with a pleasant view of the sea. The Earl of Charlemont, whose town house in Parnell Square is now the Hugh Lane Municipal Gallery of Modern Art (see pp 96–7), had his country residence near here at Marino House. He decided to build this casino, or little house, as an architectural *jeu d'esprit* beside Marino House. The architect was Sir William Chambers, of Somerset House fame, and built by Simon Vierpyl, a sculptor and builder whom Charlemont had fetched from Rome. It cost no less than £60,000, a fortune in those days.

The Casino is gorgeously decorated throughout in the most perfect detail. Servants' quarters are in a concealed basement. The chimneys are hidden in walls, thus providing a central heating system. The whole thing is deceptively large. At first glance, it looks as though it contains just a single large room whereas it has eight, on

Casino, Marino

two floors. And everywhere, it is the perfection of the decoration that draws the eye.

As the city expanded, the casino was not simply neglected, it was surrounded by unsympathetic suburban development. It now finds itself in the wrong place. As a result, what should be one of the biggest tourist attractions in the city does not draw a fraction of the visitors that it might.

Here is an immodest proposal. Move it. The Casino should be moved, block by block and stone by stone, and reconstructed in a more appropriate location. My own suggestion is the end of Sir John Rogerson's Quay as the centrepiece of the long overdue redevelopment of that area. There may be practical objections to that site. But if not there, somewhere else. This landmark building should not be condemned to its present pathetic isolation. It ought to be the anchor point of one of the renewal projects in the city.

Bull Island

Off Clontarf Road

Bus: 130 (from Lower Abbey Street)

The Bull Island is a raised sandbank on the north side of Dublin Bay. It was formed following the building of the Bull Wall — one of the two enclosing walls of the modern harbour, the other being the South Wall — in the early nineteenth century. The Bull Wall presented a barrier to the tidal movement of sand and gradually a sandbank that had been submerged at high tide formed dry land above the highest tideline.

It is now a wildlife preserve, an important bird sanctuary, a fantastic recreational amenity for the citizens of the city and a wonderful place to walk. Nowhere else do you realise the shape and topography of the bay so completely as here.

There are two access points from Clontarf Road to the island. One is across the old wooden bridge at the southern end of the island. This is accessible by bus. The causeway — about a mile further out of town — is not. The original bridge dates from 1821 and was built to give access to construction workers who were building the Bull Wall. The present structure dates from 1906. On the far side of the bridge, the large building on your left is the clubhouse of the Royal Dublin Golf Club.

The southern end of the Bull Island is the least attractive. The farther you walk along the sand or in the dunes, however, the more pleasant it becomes. The full length of the island is three miles, so it will take a fit walker two hours to walk the whole way out to Sutton Creek and back. If you are up to it, it is worth it.

Malahide and Malahide Castle

Bus: 32A (from Lower Abbey Street); 32X (Belfield to Malahide via city centre — stops in St Stephen's Green North, Dawson Street, Suffolk Street, Lower Abbey Street); 42 (from Beresford Place).

Malahide is a charming, slightly anglicised seaside village and dormitory suburb about fifteen kilometres north of the city. The village itself is pleasing but the big attraction is the nearby castle, one of the most impressive in the country. This was the home of the Talbot family, one of the oldest Hiberno-Norman families of the Pale. Their original grant of land was made by King Henry II, who died in 1189. The Talbots were here until 1975.

Most of the magnificent interior and furnishings are still *in situ*. The art collection, much of it on loan from the National Gallery, is very fine and is especially strong on Irish portraits. The 250 acres of beautifully maintained grounds are also open to the public. In the grounds, near the house, is the Fry Model Railway Museum. It is the largest and most elaborate model railway exhibition in the country. Small children of all ages love it.

Malahide Castle

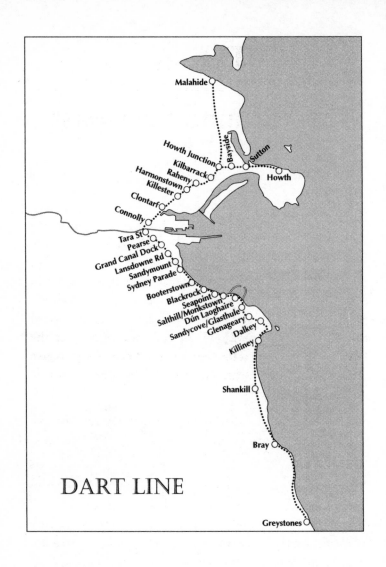

DART LINE

• Howth • Sutton • Clontarf • Booterstown and Blackrock • Dun
Laoghaire • [Sandycove] • Dalkey • Bray • Greystones

Day 6

Dart around the Coast

Day 6 Teaser
Once a church, now a museum. Where?

The DART (Dublin Area Rapid Transit) is the city's only electrified commuter line. Indeed, it is the only electrified railway in the Republic of Ireland! It was built in the 1980s, one of the few good things to happen the city in that dismal decade. It was controversial. Many rural and provincial projects that were crying out for funds envied the £120 million/G152 million that was spent on the DART. The real pity is that more has not been spent to give Dublin a proper, integrated series of commuter railway lines.

Still, the one line that there is has the advantage of hugging the bay for much of its journey. That is the big attraction for visitors.

There are 29 stations on the DART line. The itinerary today assumes that you make the journey north to south, starting at Howth and ending at Greystones, in County Wicklow. However, be warned: nobody is going to do all of this in a single day. In practice, you'll have to cherry pick. If I were you, I'd choose Howth for the morning, Dun Laoghaire, Dalkey and Killiney for the afternoon.

To get to Howth, you can either take the DART from one of the city centre stations, although this has the obvious disadvantage of making you retrace some of the journey southward, or else take the 31 or 31B bus from Lower Abbey Street or call a taxi.

Howth

Howth stands on the north side of the peninsula of the same name. It was, as near as made no difference, an island for much of its history. It is joined to the rest of Ireland only at the narrow isthmus at Sutton. To this day, all roads for the peninsula intersect at Sutton and the DART line runs through it as well.

Howth was a fishing village in medieval times, a tradition that has endured. It still boasts one of the bigger fleets in Ireland. But it is also a very expensive suburb, a marine leisure centre with its own yacht club and marina, and a favourite weekend recreational destination for Dubliners. Some of the houses on the south side of the peninsula enjoy stunning views across the bay and down the Wicklow coast.

However you travel to Howth, you'll find yourself at the harbour. It is enclosed by two piers, east and west, of which the former is the more interesting. It is on two levels and you can walk along either. The piers were built in the early nineteenth century when Howth was briefly the Dublin terminus for the Holyhead mail packet service. But the harbour was too small, shallow and prone to silting. So a new deep-water harbour was built at Dunleary — as it was then spelt — on the far side of the bay. A few years later,

Howth Harbour

Dunleary became Kingstown to honour the royal visit of King George IV, the first English monarch to visit Ireland since William of Orange and the first in history to visit for a wholly peaceful purpose.

If anywhere should have been renamed, it was Howth because it was actually here that the king first stepped ashore on Irish soil. He had been supposed to land at Dunleary, but was so drunk that it was deemed a scandal to display him thus before the loyal multitude assembled to welcome him. So they snuck him across the bay to Howth and tipped him ashore here. He left from Kingstown, as we may now call it. A hundred years later, when the British left, Kingstown reverted to its old Gaelic name — only this time properly spelt: Dun Laoghaire.

In July 1914, on the eve of the Great War, the Irish Volunteers landed arms at Howth. The Volunteers were a nationalist militia. Two years later, an extreme section of the Volunteers were the principal protagonists in the Easter Rising. Many of their weapons had been landed at Howth.

Overlooking the harbour at the eastern end is the ruined abbey of the Virgin Mary, originally a Viking foundation dated to 1042, although most of what remains to be seen here is from the fourteenth, fifteenth and sixteenth centuries. You can also see the tomb of Sir Christopher St Lawrence, 13th Baron of Howth, who died in 1462, and his wife Anna Plunket from Ratoath in Co. Meath. The St Lawrences and the Plunkets were two of the most eminent Hiberno-Norman families of the Pale.

At the western end of the village, near the railway station, is the entrance to Howth Castle. This is the ancestral home of the St Lawrence family, who still occupy it. The first member of the family known to history, Almeric, was granted these lands by King Henry II in the twelfth century. The oldest part of the present castle dates from 1564, although there have been additions in every century since. Part of the grounds have been given over to a hotel, a public golf course and a transport museum. But the gardens are still very fine, especially in May and June when the famous rhododendrons are in bloom. Speaking of which, it was up in these hillside gardens among the rhododendrons that Leopold Bloom first seduced Molly in *Ulysses*. It is the memory of that ecstatic moment that she recalls sixteen years later, on 16 June 1904, as she drifts off to sleep repeating the supreme word of affirmation, Yes.

At the far end of the harbour, on the east pier, you can hire a boat to go across to Ireland's Eye, the island that lies across the short channel. It was once the property of the archbishops of Dublin but is now a bird sanctuary. The only structure on it is a Martello Tower.

If you prefer dry land, you can walk away from the harbour, going uphill and keeping the sea on your left. After a mile or so you pick up the cliff walk which you can follow all the way round around the peninsula to Sutton (but only if you have got proper walking gear and reasonable head for heights: there are some tricky parts near the Sutton end at Redrock). Alternatively, you can just stroll to the summit without risk or much effort — it will take you about an hour.

Since today's itinerary is based on the DART, let us assume that you eventually work your way to the station to catch the DART south. The first station on the line is Sutton.

Sutton

Sutton is at the neck of the isthmus that divides Howth from the rest of Dublin. It is a middle-class suburb with nothing in particular to distinguish it. The Burrow beach, on the north side of the peninsula, is pleasant. But Sutton Creek, the northern inlet of the bay, is not particularly attractive at low tide. There is a very successful modern Catholic church on this side, built in 1973 to the design of A.D. Devane, a distinguished contrast to the usual spiritual silos put up in the suburbs in those days. There is also a pleasant walk along Strand Road with good views across the bay and towards the nearby Bull Island. But this is ideally a high-tide option. If you keep on to the very end of Strand Road, you'll meet the end of the cliff walk that began at the east pier in Howth. However, you may not wish to venture that far.

The following few stops along the DART are of little interest. The next station worth a brief stop is the one at Clontarf road.

Clontarf

Clontarf is another perfectly ordinary suburb. In the nineteenth century, it was one of the independent townships to which the middle classes fled to escape the Corporation rates. But it is a name that resonates in Irish history. The Battle of Clontarf was fought near here — actually about a mile nearer to the city, at a place now called Ballybough — in 1014. In the heroic version of Irish history, it is presented as a contest between the colonised Irish and the occupying Vikings in which the Irish under their king Brian Boru sundered the chains of slavery. The idea was to substitute the Vikings for the British in the public imagination so that we could believe that in every generation, even a millennium ago, the never-say-die Irish were resisting invaders like billy-o. In fact, it was not nearly as simple as that, being more of an Irish provincial revolt against Brian's claims to be king of all Ireland. The Vikings fought on both sides. There were lots of them locally; others – mercenaries – were shipped in from the Isle of Man specially for this gig.

The seafront at Clontarf is a pleasant walk. You are well insulated from the traffic on Clontarf Road by a linear park. As at Sutton, high tide is best. The docks are nearby, just across the channel. The linear park and walk go all the way out to the wooden bridge at the Bull Wall. Along the way, you pass the end of Castle Avenue, the eponymous castle being just a few hundred metres up there. It is now a hotel and bar, much faked up in recent years having previously been faked up in the nineteenth century by its then owners. Its origins go back to the Middle Ages but little of architectural interest remains.

At the junction of Clontarf Road and Vernon Avenue, we are at the site of the old Clontarf Sheds. These were curing sheds for herrings and other fish. They flourished in the eighteenth and early nineteenth centuries when this area was rural and the suburban development had not started. Connolly's pub, known simply as The Sheds, recalls those days.

Booterstown and Blackrock

Back to the DART. The next three stations take us through the city centre. From there, we head south. Shortly after Sydney Parade station, the line really begins to hug the coast. Booterstown is worth a stop if you want to walk on Merrion Strand or if you are an ornithologist: Booterstown Marsh is a bird sanctuary. Interestingly, it was formed by the railway. The causeway built to carry the line created the marsh in its lee.

This is the very first stretch of railway line built in Ireland. It is part of the original Dublin & Kingstown railway of 1834. The next station is Blackrock, once a popular seaside retreat full of fine villas. Even thirty years ago, while heavily suburbanised, it retained many marks of its former state. But greed and development of every kind barged in. The worst case concerned the destruction of Frescati House — where the patriot Lord Edward Fitzgerald had lived — to build a department store of stunning banality. Still, Blackrock remains a reasonably good example of a southside Victorian and Edwardian suburb: its main street, for example, is relatively unchanged over the decades.

Dun Laoghaire

The harbour made Dun Laoghaire and its rôle as principal ferry port for the Dublin region is still its most salient feature. It is also a major suburb — indeed technically it is a town in its own right — and the principal centre for yachting in the country.

The DART station was originally the terminus of the

Dublin & Kingstown Railway, the first in Ireland. The station dates to 1836, only two years after the opening of the line; the architect was John Skipton Mulvany.

The east pier is one of the most popular strolling places in Dublin, as the bourgeoisie of the south side (and others) do their Hibernian imitation of the Italian *passeggiata*. The Town Hall, on the corner of Crofton Road and Royal Marine Road, is a pleasing if derivative stone-fronted building by J.L. Robinson dating from 1880. At the top of Royal Marine Road, near the junction with George's Street, is St Michael's Church. Only the fine spire remains of the original Victorian Gothic building which was consumed in a fire in 1968. The replacement by Pearse McKenna is a minor triumph, with furniture, fixtures, fittings and stained glass by distinguished Irish artists including Imogen Stuart and Patrick Pye.

Go left into George's Street, the principal commercial thoroughfare in Dun Laoghaire. It is named for the drunken king who could not be put ashore here but had to be sent over to the north side (see Howth), where a man with a few jars on him is less likely to bother the natives. The next left takes you into Haigh's Terrace where the old Mariners' Church, dating from 1837, now houses the National Maritime Museum of Ireland. This commemorates and celebrates the long Irish maritime tradition, one that has traditionally been downplayed in a manner that is both mysterious and unusual for an island. Also in Haigh Terrace is a sculpture, Christ the King, by the Irish-American artist Andrew O'Connor, made as a memorial to the dead of the Great War.

At the end of George's Street Upper, the People's Park, now over 100 years old, retains faint echoes of Edwardian gentility.

At the end of Park Road, turn left back towards the east pier and the DART station if you are pressed for time. If not, turn right.

OPTION: SANDYCOVE

It is a ten-minute stroll along the shore of Scotsman's Bay to Sandycove. The dominant feature here is the Martello Tower in which the opening episode of Joyce's *Ulysses* is set. The book opens here, on the far south of Dublin Bay and ends in the city centre — in Eccles Street — with Molly remembering her seduction in Howth at the northern shore of the bay.

Martello Towers were built by the Admiralty as fortified lookout points during the Napoleonic Wars. The British had every reason to fear a seaborne landing by the French. A French naval commander, Thurot, actually captured and held Carrickfergus Castle in County Antrim for a while in 1760. Moreover, there was the near miss at Bantry Bay in December 1796 when a revolutionary force of 15,000 crack French troops only failed to land in undefended County Cork because of freak contrary winds. Wolfe Tone, the United Irish leader who was on board one of the ships in the uniform of a French officer, complained in his frustration that they were near enough to throw a biscuit to the shore. So London was not at all alarmist in building the Martellos, even though the invasion never came.

It was from the Admiralty that Oliver St John Gogarty, surgeon, poet, scabrous wit and the model for Malachi 'Buck' Mulligan in *Ulysses*, leased the Martello Tower in 1904. Joyce stayed there for a few nights, long enough to give it its place in literary history. It now houses a very good Joyce museum. When it opened in 1962, it was the first in Dublin. The guest of honour was Sylvia Beach, the publisher of the first edition of the great book in 1922.

Just beside the tower, there is a very interesting house built in a modernist art deco style that echoes the contours of the tower. The architect was Michael Scott, Ireland's leading modernist of the mid-century. He designed the house for himself. Just behind the tower, at Sandycove Point, is the Forty Foot which used to be men's bathing place. The point was that they swam nude there: apparently skinny dipping in the sea is very bracing. However, any men-only facility was offensive to feminist sentiment and the Forty Foot no longer enjoys its status as a male preserve.

Nearby, Bullock Harbour is a narrow creek giving shelter for small craft. The monks of St Mary's Abbey in the city had the fishing rights hereabouts and they built a castle at Bullock to protect their interests. Prior to the development of the port of Dublin and the harbour at Dun Laoghaire, this little creek was an important landing stage. It was recorded in 1660 as having the largest population on the south shore of the bay: a whole 100 adults!

Dalkey

The next stop along the line after Dun Laoghaire is Glenageary followed by Dalkey. It is pronounced 'Dawky' and is one of the most pleasing of Dublin's suburban villages. In medieval times it was a port. Now the main street is slightly in from the coast, marking the line of the landward fortifications that defended the port. The ruins of two of these are seen in Castle Street, the town's main street. A third forms part of Dalkey town hall. The modern suburb followed the railway, as did most of the developments in this corner of the city.

Dalkey Island, just off the coast, was the site of an early Christian church built by St Begnet, a local holy virgin. It was used as a goat pasture in the eighteenth century. A Georgian drinking club used to crown one of their number King of Dalkey Island each year, a happy practice that has been revived in recent decades. You can hire a boat in Coliemore Harbour to visit the island.

Don't miss Dalkey Hill. You can either take the 59 bus a few stops along Dalkey Avenue and walk up it or you can walk from Castle Street along Sorrento Road until it turns into Vico Road. One way or another, you will see the same view — just as you will see it again from the DART when you resume your journey. The point is that you can never come upon this view too often. Beyond any doubt, this is the most beautiful marine landscape in the Dublin region. The supple curve of Killiney Bay with the great Sugar Loaf in the background: it is ravishing.

Even if you can't get up here or don't have the time, don't

despair. You'll still see the view, because the DART line goes this way *en route* to Killiney, Shankill and our next stop, Bray.

Bray

Brash Bray: it is hard to love. It too was a creation of the railway, which brought watering places like this within reach of the urban multitudes. So Bray became the Blackpool of Ireland and it still retains much of its original cheery vulgarity. What has it to recommend it? A beautiful location; a fine long esplanade, at the end of which is Bray Head which is an easy climb and affords fine views; and the National Sea Life Centre, a state-of-the-art aquarium. It is also a convenient jumping-off point for various places like Powerscourt or Glendalough. But since we are on the DART today and these places, deep in County Wicklow, require a car or at least a bike, we'll leave them until tomorrow.

Greystones

The end of the line. Well, only if you must. For Greystones is rather boring, to tell the truth. It is pretty enough, I suppose, and it is everything that Bray is not: genteel, rather apologetic, restrained. It is surrounded on all sides by an explosion of suburban housing. It has a little shingle beach with nice views north to Bray Head and the Sugar Loaf but that's about it, really.

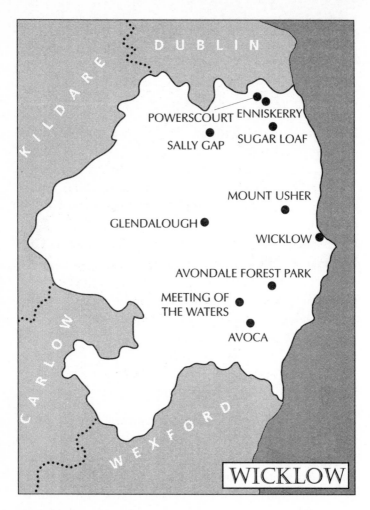

County Wicklow
• Enniskerry • Powerscourt • National Garden Exhibition Centre •
Mount Usher • Hunter's Hotel • Wicklow • Avoca • Meeting of the
Waters • Avondale • Glendalough • [Wicklow Gap] • Glenmacnass
• Sally Gap • Sugar Loaf

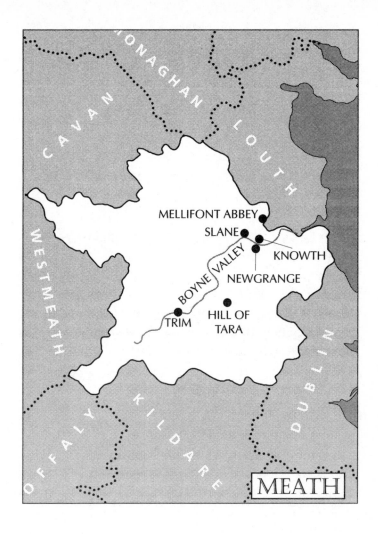

County Meath

• Trim • Hill of Tara • Boyne Valley • Slane • Newgrange • Knowth and Dowth • Battle of the Boyne • Mellifont

Day 7

Out of Town

Day 7 Teaser

He was rusticated without a degree but he made his mark none the less. Who?

Whether you go south to County Wicklow or north to County Meath, either of these out-of-town excursions can each take a whole day, and will occupy a half day at a minimum. Don't attempt to do both in the same day: you haven't a hope. Either plump for one, or at a minimum allow a half day for each and use them as alternatives to the main city itineraries.

County Wicklow

The 'Garden of Ireland' is the catch-phrase for Wicklow. In truth, it is hard to argue with it. Dublin is fortunate to have this wonderful county on its southern doorstep. You can drive from O'Connell Bridge and an hour later be standing at the Sally Gap in an upland wilderness of bog, mountain, lake and heather.

Alternatively, at the end of your hour, you could be in the pretty small-farm country near Roundwood. Or sitting in the garden of Hunter's Hotel near Ashford.

The fact is that there are three Wicklows, all close together. There are the high hills above the grass and tree line; there is a middle plateau of indifferent land but good for sheep farming; and there is a coastal littoral at sea level. The wilderness is in the centre of the county, running along the spinal cord of the Wicklow Mountains; the plateau drops off to the east; the coast is more easterly again. To the west of the mountains, the land falls away towards the plains of County Kildare.

To follow this itinerary in full, you'll need a car. First, however, some options for cyclists and walkers.

CYCLING OPTIONS

Throw your bike in the guard's van on the Wexford/Rosslare train from Connolly Station and set off. In County Wicklow, there are stops at Bray, Greystones, Wicklow town, Rathdrum and Arklow. From Bray, you can cover Enniskerry, Powerscourt and Glencree. Greystones is best for the Sugar Loaf, Calary and Roundwood. Alight at Wicklow for Ashford, Mount Usher Gardens, the Devil's Glen or the coast south of Wicklow Head. Rathdrum is for Avondale, Avoca, the Meeting of the Waters, the Vale of Clara and Glendalough. Arklow gives you options in the south Wicklow/north Wexford area.

You can easily work out detailed itineraries for yourself, based on return train times to Dublin. And of course there is no reason why you should not get out at one station and return from another — as long as you remember to buy a return ticket to the destination farther away from Dublin!

WALKING OPTIONS

Wicklow is a walker's paradise. If you only have a day, don't despair. You can easily do a return day trip into the heart of Wicklow and still have time for a satisfying walk. The first thing is to plan an itinerary.

You can take the train, as with the cyclists.

In addition, you can give a little custom to Bus Eireann, the national bus company. They run a service from Busaras in Dublin to Wexford-Rosslare that stops in Ashford and Wicklow town.

Moreover, Dublin Bus runs the 184 service from Bray DART station to Greystones, Delgany and Newtownmountkennedy (the longest place-name in Ireland, by the way). Then there is one of the country's better-kept secrets, the St Kevin's Bus, a private bus service that leaves the College of Surgeons in St Stephen's Green at 11.30 a.m. each day and delivers you to Glendalough.

Take your pick. Once you have decided what you want, you can consult one of three excellent books. First there is Joss Lynam's *Easy Walks Near Dublin*, a guide to forty walks within an hour of the city centre — the majority of them in Wicklow. Then there is *Walk Guide: East of Ireland* by Jean Boydell and Miriam Joyce McCarthy, again with lots of Wicklow options although generally of a slightly more demanding standard than Lynam. Finally, if you go for the Wicklow Way option — either starting from Marlay Park or joining it further down — the standard guide is J.B. Malone's *Complete Wicklow Way: a step-by-step guide*. The late J.B. Malone was the prime mover behind the Wicklow Way.

Between these books and the various transport options, you should be able to plan a good day's walking.

Enniskerry

From the M11, take the R117 for about 6.5 kilometres. Enniskerry was the estate village for Powerscourt Demesne and it has the neat, quaint sense of good order that is characteristic of estate villages throughout Ireland. Many Irish villages and small towns give off an air of random settlement, without any sense of historic planning. Estate villages, on the other hand, usually reflect the proprietorial pride of their landlord patrons. This can express itself in a number of ways: statuary and other public monuments; classical buildings; a uniform architectural style; cut stone work. Enniskerry is the perfect introduction to Powerscourt, in whose shadow it stands.

Powerscourt

Powerscourt was the demesne of the viscounts of the same name, whose town house in South William Street we have met already (p. 26). It was completed in 1741 to a design by Richard Castle. Tragically, it was gutted by fire in 1974 and only the shell remains.

After the arrival of the Normans, these lands came into the possession of the le Poer (Power) family. After the Tudor reconquest of Ireland, the estate passed to the Wingfields who took the title Powerscourt in deference to the historic connection with the former owners.

Powerscourt

It is the gardens that are the big attraction. First laid out in the eighteenth century but much altered in the nineteenth, they are approached through wrought-iron gates that were once in Bamberg cathedral in Germany. The superb terraces in front of the house, with their breathtaking view onto the Dargle Valley and the Great Sugar Loaf, were laid out by Daniel Robertson in the nineteenth century. It appears that Robertson's working methods were eccentric, to say the least. According to a leaflet guide published to the gardens in 1948 and quoted by Maurice Craig in his classic, *Dublin 1660–1860*, he 'was wheeled about the place in a wheelbarrow grasping a bottle of sherry. When the sherry was finished Mr Robertson ended his designing for the day'.

The grounds are magnificently laid out and beautifully maintained. They support a huge variety of mature trees and there are many lovely walks. There is also a Japanese Garden. At a distance of almost 5 kilometres from the house, the Powerscourt Waterfall is the other great attraction. It is the highest waterfall in Britain or Ireland, falling 121 metres. If you prefer to drive to the waterfall, you can do so separately by road: there is another entrance to the demesne there.

National Garden Exhibition Centre

Heading south on the N11, you pass Great Sugar Loaf at the village of Kilmacanogue and then cut through the defile known as the Glen of the Downs. Turn left at Kilpeddar and follow the signs for the National Garden Exhibition Centre. There are twenty different garden types on display here, laid out by some of Ireland's leading horticultural designers. They range from an Oriental garden to an Irish rural garden, a Mediterranean garden and a conifer garden. There is a contemplative garden, a light and shade garden and an acid soil garden. And much more.

Mount Usher Gardens

Let us stay with the garden theme just for the moment. A few kilometres further down the N11, the village of Ashford boasts one of the finest gardens in Ireland. Mount Usher is spread over 8 hectares on either side of the River Vartry. It contains over 5,000 varieties of trees, shrubs and plants collected by four generations of the Walpole family who lived in Mount Usher House. Many of the more exotic varieties are unique to Mount Usher – at least in an Irish context. This is a truly beautiful place.

Hunter's Hotel

Also beside the Vartry, a few miles further downstream at Newrath Bridge, is Hunter's Hotel. This gem, an old Georgian coaching inn, is beautiful in itself. It is well worth stopping for some refreshment here. They do a good lunch of decent, traditional, no-nonsense food. And then there is the garden with its uncompromising notice that states: 'Ladies and gentlemen will not and others may not pick the flowers in this garden'. It is a delight to sit in, as guests of the hotel are welcome to do, not least because it isn't grand or imposing or over-formal – just a well-loved and tended country garden.

Wicklow

Wicklow town itself is of Viking origin, although they were

elbowed aside here, as so many other places, by the later arrival of the Normans. Black Castle, now ruinous, dates back to 1178 and stands on the coast just outside the town.

The Wicklow Gaol is the town's newest tourist attraction. It was open for business from 1702 until 1924. Then followed years of neglect. Recently it has been thoroughly renovated and restored and now offers an up-to-the-minute interactive guide to local and Irish history through reconstructions of the people and events to which the gaol was witness.

Wicklow Head, a few kilometres south of the town, is the most easterly point in the Republic of Ireland.

Avoca and the Meeting of the Waters

The little village of Avoca was formerly a centre of the Wicklow copper mining industry, now discontinued. You can still see the worked out excavations in the area, with their distinctive ochre-coloured spoil. The village itself is extremely picturesque and has become famous in recent years as the setting for the television series *Ballykissangel*, a major commercial success particularly in Britain.

Avoca has consolidated its new-found fame and even has its own website to advertise itself to the world. However, www.avoca.com may be bang up date in its technology but its message is all traditional Oirish, complete with leprechauns, fairies, a colleen called Tara and other manifestations of Paddywhackery. Harmless innocent fun, of course.

Just north of the village, on the road to Rathdrum (R752)

is the Meeting of the Waters. It is simply the confluence of the Avonmore and Avonbeg rivers, both of which flow down from the high hills in the centre of the county. The names are simply anglicised forms of Irish words that mean big river (Avonmore) and little river (Avonbeg). As we saw earlier (p. 94, Millennium Fountain), the Irish word for a river is Amhain, pronounced Ow en, with the first syllable rhyming with 'now'. In the case of the Liffey, this was anglicised as Anna; more usually it came out as Avon, as in Stratford-on. It is pleasing to think that the name of the river in Shakespeare's home town is a borrowing from Gaelic. It is good to see some two-way cultural traffic.

The Meeting of the Waters is indelibly associated with another writer, Thomas Moore. For most of the nineteenth century and much of the twentieth, Tom Moore was regarded as Ireland's national poet. His verse, set to airs collected by the collector Edward Bunting, provided a staple repertoire of sentimental patriotic ballads. *Moore's Melodies* were once sung in every house in Ireland that had an upright piano. He was thoroughly excoriated by later generations — Joyce wrote quite viciously about him — and is now out of fashion, perhaps for good. It was here, at the Meeting of the Waters, that Moore wrote one of his more famous ballads:

> There is not in this wide world a valley so sweet
> As that vale in whose bosom the bright waters meet...

and so on. To be fair the Vale of Avoca is lovely and this spot, although it is a tourist trap, is peaceful and relaxing.

Nearby is the village of Rathdrum and just outside it is

Avondale, a small Georgian country house. It was the home of Charles Stewart Parnell (1846-91), the nationalist leader who inspired a generation and put Irish home rule seriously on the political map for the first time. Although Irish independence had to wait for thirty years after Parnell's death, he had put most of the structures in place which made it possible. Some historians argue that he created a state in embryo, just waiting the appropriate moment to be born. He was a mass of contradictions: a Protestant landlord leading a movement of Catholic tenants; a cold, aloof man who was none the less adored by the Irish people; an Irish nationalist leader with a violent aversion to the colour green; a poor speaker in a country drunk on oratory. Yet no one who came in contact with him ever forgot him. Joyce and Yeats were both hypnotised by him; Gladstone thought him the greatest political leader he had encountered in a long career.

The Parnells had been prominent in Irish public life for generations. They were a leading county family and Avondale, although small by country house standards, was still a very grand residence indeed in a poor country barely emerging from the grip of the Great Famine (1845-52). Parnell was educated at Cambridge from which he was sent down without a degree. It is speculated that this turned him against the English. What is certain is that he never played by English rules. He cheated at cricket, that most English of games in which chivalrous good sportsmanship was at a premium. And he cheated at English politics, refusing to play by the rules of the House of Commons by shameless filibustering. The guillotine system of restricting debates to a set time period dates from Parnell's time: it was a measure

Glendalough

introduced in despair at the serial filibustering of Irish members under Parnell's leadership. English members, even the most awkward, could be trusted to play by the rules. Not Parnell.

Glendalough

The most famous tourist venue in County Wicklow lies about 12 kilometres north of Rathdrum. To reach it you travel along the road that skirts the lovely Vale of Clara, passing the tiny hamlet of Clara deep in the valley on your right with its distinctive white church. Turn left at the village of Laragh and in a few minutes you are in Glendalough.

If you have followed this itinerary so far, you'll be aware that you are now encountering the high mountains — high, at least, by Irish standards — for the first time. Since Avoca, you have been on the middling plateau. Glendalough — the valley of the twin lakes — is a different landscape.

It must have been suitably remote when St Kevin, the sixth-century anchorite, established his spiritual base here. The monastic settlement grew with time until it encompassed seven churches and a round tower. The Vikings attacked the site in the eleventh century and the English of Dublin at the end of the fourteenth. By the middle of the sixteenth century, Glendalough was a ruin.

The first thing to be said about Glendalough is that it is very beautiful. The great sweep of Camaderry on the right and Lugduff and Mullacor on the left give a dramatic definition to the Upper Lake on the valley floor.

Immediately behind the Royal Hotel, you can see the old gatehouse to the monastic settlement, the only surviving structure of its kind in the country. The nearby round tower is well preserved, the roof having been restored using the original stones. Most of the other ecclesiastical buildings on the site date from the tenth to twelfth centuries. Look out especially for St Kevin's Church (sometimes called St Kevin's Kitchen), a beautifully rendered little oratory with a steeply pitched roof and a bell tower done in the style of a small round tower.

OPTION: THE WICKLOW GAP

If you are pressed for time and need to return to Dublin, there is still a chance to experience some of the Wicklow uplands. Just outside Glendalough, on the road back to Laragh, there is a very sharp dog-leg left-hand turn that will take you uphill towards the Wicklow Gap. This is a clearing in the wild high country, between the mountains of Camaderry and Tonelagee, through which a road is punched to give quick access to the lowlands of west Wicklow. The road (R756) takes you up over the Gap — wild, rock-strewn country, this, an hour from O'Connell Bridge! — and along a bog road where stands of conifers gradually become more plentiful. Turn right onto the R758 signposted for Valleymount and Blessington. It is a direct route from Blessington back to the city, but at least you won't have left Wicklow without experiencing something of its majestic wilderness.

Glenmacnass

From Glendalough, return to Laragh and take the R115 towards the Sally Gap. You'll soon notice that you are above the tree line and heading relentlessly uphill towards the head of a long valley. This is Glenmacnass, a glacial leftover drained by the river of the same name which rises a few miles to the north on the slopes of Mullaghcleevaun. You can park at the head of the valley and walk to the edge of the waterfall — be careful: if you go over the side, that will be the end of you — to what is one of the most stirring places in Ireland. The roar of the water tumbling over the side, the long valley with its small, tenacious farms far below on the valley bottom and the sheer wildness of the place: it is wonderful.

Sally Gap

Continue north on the narrow R115. You are now in the high Wicklow mountains, surrounded on all sides by bog and heather. The colours can be fantastic, especially when the heather is in bloom, and the views likewise. For this is a dramatic landscape by any measure. It is devoid of people: there is no living of any sort to be had up here. But the contours of the hills, the way they catch the changing light, and the changing cloud formations overhead: all combine to invest this lonely place with its own special aura.

The road you are travelling on is marked on Ordnance Survey maps as a military road and so it is. It was built by the British following the 1798 Rising to allow hot pursuit of rebels who had retreated to the high hills following the collapse of the rebellion further south.

The Sally Gap is just a crossroads. It is a bit of an anticlimax if you were expecting a dramatic, romantic defile as the name suggests. The name is a mystery. The word 'sally' in Hiberno-English usually means 'willow', from the Irish *saileach* (pron. sal-yock). Thus Yeats's 'Down in the Sally Gardens'. But, as you can see, there isn't a willow in sight up here — or any tree at all.

Turn right at the Sally Gap onto the R759. The road takes you down towards the central plateau. There are dramatic views above Lough Tay and Luggala (pronounced Lugga-law) before you join the R755 northbound across Calary heading towards the Sugar Loaf.

Great Sugar Loaf

The Great Sugar Loaf, like most mountains of its kind, is a long extinct volcano. It draws much of its drama from its relative isolation, for it stands on the edge of the central plateau overlooking the flat coastal area of the county to the east. If you have any time and energy left, you can leave the R755 just to the south of the mountain. A right-hand turn takes you on to a narrow country road and soon you reach a car park on your left. If you want to climb the Sugar Loaf, it is a fairly easy ascent from this side, with just a little rough scrambling beneath the summit. It is a popular family climb, this, and it is not unusual to see quite small children making the ascent with their parents. You will be up and down in an hour. Needless to say, you'll be rewarded with splendid views from the summit: Tonduff, Maulin and Djouce mountains in the high hills to the west; the flat land at your feet, Bray and Greystones not far away and the Irish Sea in the background.

Once back in the car, you can stay on the little road. There is a fine descent with splendid views out to sea as you drop off the plateau to sea level to rejoin the main N11 northwards to the city.

OPTION: DAY TRIP TO WEXFORD

If you want an alternative to Counties Wicklow or Meath, you can take a day trip to Wexford by train. This is simply the most pleasant rail journey in Ireland. At Connolly Station, head for the Rosslare train. Rosslare is the ferryport a little south of Wexford itself, but all Rosslare trains stop at Wexford. Key tip: sit on the left-hand side of the train facing the engine for the best views.

The first part of the journey is along the DART line as far as Greystones, including the stunning views of Killiney Bay between Dalkey and Bray. South of Greystones, the line hugs the coast — almost literally — until Wicklow town. Here the line swings inland in a great loop through lovely wooded countryside, past Avoca and Woodenbridge, before briefly re-joining the coast at Arklow.

From there, it is inland again through the pleasant countryside of north County Wexford. South of Enniscorthy, the mid-county market town, the line runs along the banks of the River Slaney which eventually opens into a great estuary as you approach Wexford.

Alight here and spend a few hours exploring this fascinating town, with its extra narrow Main Street. Originally of Viking foundation (the name is derived from the Norse 'Weiss fiord'), it is full of historical curiosity and has some fine old buildings. You can pass a pleasant few hours here before heading back to the station for the return train to Dublin.

County Meath

Part of this itinerary spills over into County Louth but most of it is in County Meath, so we'll stick with that headline.

Meath is popularly called the Royal County, because it was the seat of the so-called high kings of Ireland. In fact, they were simply provincial kings, although still very powerful. Meath was rich then as it is today. This is good, flat, fertile land, as different from the poor soil of upland Wicklow as you can imagine. Whoever ruled hereabouts was someone to be reckoned with.

Drive north from Dublin on the N3, turning left on to the R154 for Trim.

Trim
When the Normans came to Ireland in the late twelfth century, they made a dramatic impact. Their superior military technology enabled them to grab much of the best land, especially in the east of the country. What they now held, they defended by building massive fortified houses and castles. These were easily the largest structures built in Ireland until that time. There is no more dramatic example than Trim Castle. It was the largest Norman fortress in Ireland, its moat fed by the waters of the Boyne.

It was founded by Hugh de Lacy, one of the very first Norman lords, in 1173. The present structure was rebuilt in the early thirteenth century, being completed in 1224. The keep is almost 23 metres high, accommodating three floors. The great hall is on the ground floor. The exterior walls, in a remarkably fine state of repair, are over 500 metres long.

The castle was just one part — albeit the largest part — of an integrated Norman settlement. There were Dominican and Franciscan friaries, an Augustinian priory, a hospital, a convent and a parish church.

One can easily imagine the intimidating effect a defensive fortification like this, looming massively above the Boyne, would have had on potential enemies. Until the invention of artillery, Trim was impregnable. In later centuries, the castle was captured on a number of occasions in the ebb and flow of Irish military affairs. None the less, it remains the single most impressive early Norman structure in the country.

Some visitors will recognise it as the setting for parts of the movie *Braveheart*, which were shot here.

Hill of Tara
From Trim, it is a short journey to Tara along a series of back roads.

There is probably no single place in Ireland with a greater accretion of legend, tall tales and romance than Tara. It is remembered as the seat of the high kings of Ireland, the centre of a law-bound Irish state in its golden age. This, I am sorry to say, is all nonsense. There were no high kings ruling a unified Irish kingdom. Gaelic Ireland was famously divided into some large provincial kingdoms and many minor ones, in a constant state of instability. Minor wars, fought for cattle and plunder, were endemic.

The high kingship was a myth required by nationalists in the nineteenth century, so that they could argue that Ireland had been a unified nation before the English came. Therefore, the struggle for the nation was simply a fight to recover ancient liberties. Good spin, bad history.

So what was Tara? It was an ancient religious site, later the seat of the kings of Meath. The kings of Meath were indeed, as often as not, the most powerful provincial kings in Ireland. But that is not the same as being kings of all Ireland. Its influence as a royal centre was already on the wane by the eighth century.

What you see before you is fine hillside, the top of which commands splendid views across the plains of Meath. This was a naturally defensible place. There are no spectacular ruins or remains here, nothing dramatic like the Rock of Cashel in County Tipperary, another hilly fortress in flat country which was the seat of the kings of Munster. Nevertheless, there are things of interest. The King's Rath, or royal enclosure, was here. You can still trace the earthworks that enclosed it and the mounds within it, one the royal throne and the other known as Cormac's House. Near the northern end of the King's Rath is the Mound of the Hostages.

The Mound of the Hostages is the supposed site of the Lia

Fáil, or coronation stone of the kings of Tara. According to legend, a sixth-century king of Tara lent it to his brother who was king of Scotland. It was never returned but instead became the Stone of Scone, the coronation stone of the kings of Scotland. England's King Edward I — 'the hammer of the Scots' — took it away to London in 1297 after a punitive expedition in which he laid waste the lowlands. It stayed in Westminster Abbey until a few years ago when the rising tide of Scots nationalism had it returned to Scotland. All of which suggests that it is time we asked the Scots for our stone back.

The standing stone beside Cormac's House is referred to as the Lia Fáil. But it is not. It is a commemorative stone marking the burial place of rebels killed here during a minor battle in the 1798 Rising. Nearby is a hideous statue of St Patrick.

Boyne Valley

It is little surprise that the earliest records of deeply civilised life are to be found here, in the valley of the river Boyne, concentrated in a remarkably small area. The richness of this land made it a natural site for agricultural and pastoral settlement. What we come to see in the Boyne Valley are the very dramatic remains of an ancient, settled culture.

Slane

From Navan, take the N51 east to Slane. If you are coming direct from Dublin, take the N2 north. This is another estate town, as one can immediately see from the four tall, somewhat gaunt classical houses that stand uniformly at the corners of the crossroads, set at an angle of 45 degrees to the road. Nearby Slane Castle is the ancestral home of the Lords Mountcharles and it is still occupied by them. Despite a disastrous fire in 1991, the castle has been restored. The present owner, Lord Henry Mountcharles, has shown real imagination and ingenuity in order to make ends meet. Most famously, he stages a huge open-air rock concert in the grounds of the castle each August, regularly attracting some of the world's top acts.

Just north of the village is the Hill of Slane where legend has it that St Patrick lit the first Paschal candle in Ireland to proclaim the light of Christianity to the heathen. There are remains here of a very ancient ecclesiastical settlement which survived raids by Vikings, Normans, Gaelic chieftains and Cromwellians alike before finally being abandoned in the early eighteenth century.

Return to the centre of Slane and turn left along the N51 towards Drogheda. In due course, you will see the signposts for Newgrange.

Newgrange

No matter where you travel, there are some sights that are marked 'must not miss'. In the greater Dublin area, Newgrange is one such. It is a Neolithic (stone age) passage grave, one of a series at this site formed by a long bend in the River Boyne. In Irish, the whole necropolis is known as Bru na Boinne (the bank of the Boyne) but the people who created Newgrange and the other passage graves did not speak Irish. These ancient people predated the Gaelic-

Newgrange

speaking Celts by thousands of years. We don't know what language they spoke.

Bru na Boinne has been described as Ireland's Valley of the Kings. In all, there are over thirty passage graves in the Boyne Valley, of which Knowth, Dowth and Newgrange are the most celebrated. Of these, Newgrange is the one most thoroughly excavated. A passage grave comprises a circular stone tumulus or cairn containing a central passageway leading to the actual burial chamber.

Newgrange dates from about 2500 BC. The people who built it were farmers, alert to the changes of season and the position of the sun. This is evident from the light box situated above the entrance to the central passageway. It is angled so precisely that it catches the dawn sunlight on the day of the winter solstice and allows it to shine the length of the entire passageway, illuminating the burial chamber for about twenty minutes. On no other day in the year does this happen. In order to calibrate the orientation of the light box so precisely, its designers had to be skilled in the accurate observation of the heavens. The winter solstice is a sacred day in many cultures, marking the point in the year when the light begins its long return journey towards us. It is the moment of rebirth.

The light box is the most dramatic single feature of Newgrange but the entire tumulus, now brilliantly excavated and presented to visitors, is a marvel. It is one of the most sensational ancient constructions in northern Europe. Again, the sophistication displayed by the designers and craftsmen who built it is astonishing. The circular cairn enclosing the passage grave is itself more than 100 metres in diameter. The roofing stones contain shallow, concave channels which carry rainwater safely away to the edge of the cairn: Neolithic guttering, and still very efficient three and a half thousand years later. The beautiful spiral designs on the exterior stones testify to the skill of the craftsmen who placed them there.

The Bru na Boinne Visitor Centre is a model of its kind. It has an up-to-the-minute interactive display, including a simulation of the experience in the burial chamber at the winter solstice.

Knowth and Dowth

Knowth is the second major passage grave in the Bru na Boinne complex. In the view of one authority, it is 'patently the most important of the passage tomb complexes so far excavated in Ireland'. It contains two passage graves, one of which is cruciform in shape.

It is the largest of all the passage graves in the Boyne Valley and it has no less than seventeen satellite tombs adjacent. One of the most startling discoveries at Knowth is a map of the moon, carved in stone, in one of the passages. Previously, the oldest known map of the moon was that made by Leonardo da Vinci in the early sixteenth century.

Direct access to Knowth is not possible. However, there are guided visitor tours from the Bru na Boinne Visitor Centre.

Dowth is only one of the three passage graves not open to the public. However, it is possible to drive close to the site and see it. It contains two passage graves, one of them aligned to the setting sun at the winter solstice.

Battle of the Boyne

The most famous battle in Irish history was fought a short distance away from Newgrange. The site is well signposted.

On 12 July 1690, the armies of King James II and King William III met here. James was the legitimate king, a Stuart and a Catholic. He had also produced a Catholic heir. But England and Scotland (he was king of both) were Protestant kingdoms and they feared persecution. Therefore they overthrew James in what was known as the Glorious Revolution. It was simple usurpation, but it worked. The old line that says 'if treason prosper none dare call it treason' was never truer.

With the larger island having welcomed William as king, James retreated to Ireland whose Catholic majority made it a natural stronghold for him. Eventually William followed and the two kings fought for the three kingdoms (England, Scotland and Ireland) at the Boyne. William won, a victory that is still celebrated annually in Protestant Ulster to this day.

Mellifont

To reach Mellifont Abbey, one of the finest Cistercian ruins in Ireland, continue on the N51 towards Drogheda. Before you reach the town, you will see a signpost for Mellifont bidding you to turn left. Take this turn, follow the signs and you are there.

Mellifont was the first Cistercian abbey in Ireland. The Cistercians were a self-consciously imperial order who brought the reforming uniformity of the continental church to Ireland. The formal disposition of the architectural elements at Mellifont, obvious even in its ruinous state, symbolised their larger purpose.

The abbey dates to 1140. Its founder, St Malachy, had been a disciple of St Bernard of Clairvaux — the greatest of the Cistercian theologians and famous as a founder of monasteries. St Malachy emulated his master's example: within thirty years of the foundation of Mellifont, a further twenty-four Cistercian houses had been established in Ireland. Mellifont was destroyed in 1539 at the time of the dissolution of the monasteries.

The plan of the abbey followed a conventional Cistercian model: church to the north, chapter house to the south. The most conspicuous feature of these ruins is the lavabo or washing place, an octagonal structure on the south side of the cloister. It dates from about 1200. The gatehouse is also impressive.

Return to Dublin via Drogheda and the N1.

Index

Figures in italics indicate map references or illustrations

Abbey Presbyterian Church
    101
Abbey Street 90, 92, 106
Abbey Theatre *x,* 106–09
Act of Union viii, 12, 26, 28
All-Night Stores xv
Aras an Uachtarain 71
Arbour Hill *60,* 75–6
Ark, The (children's theatre) 43
Avoca *142,* 151–5
Avondale *142,* 153–5

Baggot Street ix, 119
Bank of Ireland *xxxii,* 10–12
Barber Shop xvi
Barrington, Sir Jonah 22–3
Battle of Clontarf 134–5
Battle of the Boyne 168
Beauty salon xvii
Beckett, Samuel10, 104
Bewley's xxvii, 14, *15*
Blackrock *128,* 136
Blessington Street Basin *86,* 98
Bloomsday xxviii
Bluecoat School, *see*
    Incorporated Law Society
Book of Kells 6–7

Booterstown *128,* 136
Bord Failte xiii
Botanic Gardens *110,* 120
Boyne Valley *143,* 163–9
Bray xiii, *128,* 141, 145
Brazen Head, the *56*
Bull Island *110,* 124–5
Burke, Edmund 2, 8, 78
Busaras 83

Capel Street 63, 88
Capel Street Bridge *58,* 63
Carson, Edward 9
Casino, Marino 95, 122–4, *123*
Castle, Richard 4, *5,* 94, 106
Central Bank *38,* 39–40, *41*
Ceol (Traditional Music
    Centre) 77
Chambers, Sir William 113,
    122
Charlemont, Lord (James
    Caulfield) 95
Chester Beatty Library 57–8
Chimney, the. *see* Smithfield
Christ Church Cathedral ix, *38,*
    46–8, *47*
Church Street 78

City Hall 38, 58–9

Civic Offices 38, 44–6, 63

Clarence Hotel 43, 63

Clarendon Street (see also St Teresa's Church) 14, 26

Clery's 92

Clontarf 128, 134–5

Coffee shop xvii

College Green xxxii, 10–12

Collins' Barracks 75

Comyn, John 48

Connolly Station xiii

Cope Street 42

Coppinger Row 26

Croppies' Acre 75

Crown Alley 42

Curved Street 42

Custom House 60, 81–3

Dalkey xiii, 128, 140–41

Dame Street 1, 39

Davis, Thomas 9, 12, 117

Dawson Street 36–7

de Valera, Eamon 68

Deane & Woodward (architects) 5, 17, 34

Delany, Edward 12, 17

Delicatessen xvii

Dorset Street 98, 100

Douglas Hyde Gallery 7

Dowth 143, 167

Drimnagh Castle 110, 113

Drury Street 27

Dublin Castle vii, 38, 56–8

Dublin Civic Museum 26

Dublin Tourism Information Office xiii, 26

Dublin Writers' Museum 86, 97–8

Dublinia 48

Duke Street 37

Dun Laoghaire xiii, 128, 136–8

Earl Street 92

Earlsfort Terrace 18, 21

Eccles Street 100

Eden Quay 82

Ely Place 28

Emergency telephone numbers xiv

Emmet, Robert 8, 68

Enniskerry 142, 145, 147

Exchequer Street 24

Fade Street 24

Findlater's Church, see Abbey Presbyterian Church

Fishamble Street 44, 45, 63

Fitzwilliam Square xxxii, 21, 28–9

Fleet Street 42

Floozie in the Jacuzzi, the, see Millennium Fountain

Foley, John Henry 2, 12, 49, 88–9

Foot massage xvii

Four Courts 66, 78–81, 79

Francis Street 38, 53–4

Fry Model Railway Museum, Malahide 126
Furry Glen 73–4

Gaiety Theatre 23–4
Gallagher Gallery, *see* Royal Hibernian Academy
Gandon, James 11, 80, 81, 83, 88, 101
Garden of Remembrance *86*, *95*, 97–8
Gardiner Street 83, 87
Gardiner, Luke 87
Gate Theatre *86*, 102–05
Gay and Lesbian scene xxix
General Post Office 92
George IV, drunken king 132
Georgian squares 27–37
Glasnevin Cemetery 120
Glendalough *142*, *154*, 155–6
Glenmacnass 157
Gogarty, Oliver St John 10, 139
Goldsmith, Oliver 2,8
Government Buildings *xxxii*, 30
Grafton Street ix, *xxxii*, 13–16
Grand Canal ix, 21, 32, 98, 118
Grattan, Henry 8, 12, 63
Great Sugar Loaf 158
Gresham Hotel 92
Greystones *128*, 141, 145
Guinness 52
Guinness Brewery 52, *54*
Guinness Storehouse ix, 52–3

Halfpenny Bridge 42, 62–3
Hand knits xviii
Handel, George Frideric 44
Harcourt Street *xxxii*, 22–3
Hatch Street 21, 22
Henrietta Street *86*, 100
Heuston Station ix, xiii, 60, 62, 65–6
House of Lords (Bank of Ireland) 10–12
Howth *128*, 130–34
Howth Harbour 130–32, *131*
Hugh Lane Municipal Gallery *86*, *95*, 96–7, 99
Huguenot Cemetery 27–8
Hume Street 17
Hunter's Hotel 144,150
Hurling xxvii
Hyde, Douglas 9, 23

Incorporated Law Society 76
International Financial Services Centre (IFSC) *60*, 84, 85
Irish Film Centre 44
Irish Jewish Museum 118
Irish Museum of Modern Art (IMMA) 66–7
Irish Tourist Board (Bord Failet) xiii
Irish Traditional Music Centre. *see* Ceol
Irish Whiskey Corner 77–8

James Joyce Centre 101–02

Jameson's Distillery 77
John's Lane Church 55
Johnston, Francis 57, 68, 71, 92, 100
Joyce, James viii, xxix, 1, 19, 20, 56, 65, 77, 102, 138–9
Juice bars xviii

Kavanagh, Patrick 118
Kildare Street xxxii, 34
Kildare Street Club 17, 34
Killiney xiii
Kilmainham Jail xxx, 60, 67–8
King's Hospital, see Incorporated Law Society
King's Inns 86, 100–01
Knowth 143, 167

Larkin, James 93
Leeson Street xxxii, 21
Leinster House xxxii, 31, 34–5
Liberties, the 51–6
Liberty Hall 82–3
Loopline Bridge 82
Luggage Repairs xvi

Mac Liammóir, Micheál 103
Magazine Fort 72–3
Malahide 125–6
Malahide Castle 110
Mansion House 36–7
Maritime Museum, see National Maritime Museum
Market Arcade 24

Marlborough Street 105
Marsh's Library 38, 50–51
Martello Towers 133, 138
Mathew, Fr Theobald 64, 93
Meath Street 38, 53
Meath, County 160–63
Meeting House Square 42–3
Meeting of the Waters 142, 152
Mellifont 168–9
Menswear xviii
Merchant's Arch 42
Merrion Square xxxii, 21, 30–34, 33
Messiah, see Handel
Millennium Bridge 63
Millennium Fountain 94–5
Model Railway Museum, see under Fry
Molesworth Street xxxii, 35–6
Moore, Henry 4, 20, 152
Mount Jerome Cemetery 117
Mount Usher Gardens 142, 150
Mountjoy Square 86, 101–02

National College of Art and Design 53
National Concert Hall 19, 21–2
National Gallery xxxii, 30, 32–4
National Garden Exhibition Centre 149–50
National Library xxxii, 30, 35
National Maritime Museum 137

National Maternity Hospital 21, 32

National Museum *xxxii*, 30, 35, *60*, 74

Natural History Museum 30

Newgrange 164–7, *165*

Newman House 18–19

Nightlife xxxi

Normans 46, 147, 151, 160–61

North Great George's Street *86*, 101–02

North Quays 60

O'Casey, Sean 104, 107, 108

O'Connell Street ix, *86*, 88–94, *91*

O'Connell, Daniel 31, 88–9, 93, 121

Off-licences xv

Ordnance Survey 74

Ormond Quay 82

Oxmantown 87

Palestrina Choir 106

Parliament Street 43, 58, 63

Parnell Square ix, *86*, 95, 97, 101

Parnell Street 92, 94, 95

Parnell, Charles Stewart 68, 121, 153–4

Pearse Street *5*

Pembroke Road 119

Pepper Cannister Church (St Stephen's) 31, *33*

Phoenix Column 71–2

Phoenix Park ix, *60*, 68–74

Poolbeg lighthouse xxxviii

Portobello 118

Post Offices xv

Powerscourt *142*, 145, 147–9, *148*

Powerscourt Townhouse Centre 26

Pro-Cathedral 105–06

Prospect Cemetery. *see* Glasnevin

Pubs xix–xxiii

Queen Street 76

Rainy-Day options xxxi

Rathfarnham Castle *110*, 113, 114

Rathgar *110*, 115–17

Rathmines *110*, 115–17

Restaurants xxiv–xxvii

Rotunda *86*, 94–5

Roundwood 144, 145

Royal Canal 98

Royal College of Physicians 34

Royal College of Surgeons in Ireland 10–20

Royal Dublin Golf Club 125

Royal Dublin Society (RDS) *110*, 111–12

Royal Hibernian Academy 28

Royal Hospital 66–7

Royal Irish Academy 36

Russell, George (AE) 31

Sally Gap *142*, 144, 157–8
Sandwich bar xviii
Sandycove *128*, 138–9
Scott, Michael 83, 106
Shaw, (George) Bernard 17, 32–4, 118
Shelbourne Hotel 17, 27
Shoe Repairs xv
Slane *143*, 163–4
Smithfield *60*, 76–8
South City Markets 27
South Great George's Street xxxii, 23, 27
South King Street 23–4
South Quays 60, 62
South William Street 24, 26
Souvenirs xvi
St Ann's Church 36
St Audeon's Arch 56
St Audeon's churches 55–6
St Bartholomew's Church 112
St Catherine's Church, Thomas Street 53
St George's Church 100
St Mary's Abbey 119
St Mary's Hospital 72
St Michan's Church *60*, 78
St Patrick's Cathedral *38*, 48–50
St Stephen's Green ix, *xxxii*, 13, 16–20
St Teresa's Church, Clarendon Street 26
Stephenson, Sam 40, 45–6
Stoneybatter 76
Street market xviii
Strongbow (Richard de Clare) 46
Sunlight Chambers 63
Sutton *128*, 134
Swift, Jonathan 49–50, 72
Synge, John Millington 10, 107, 108

Tailor's Hall 55
Tara *143*, 161–3
Temple Bar ix, 39–44, *38, 63*
Tone, Theobald Wolfe 8, 17, *36, 55*
Tourist Information Centre xiv
Tourist Offices xiii, xiv, 26
Transport xiv
Trim *143*, 160–61
Trinity College vii, ix, *xxxii*, 1–10, *3*
Tyrone House 106

Ulysses 1, 4, 32, *56*, 75–6, 82, 92, 100, 121, 133, 138, 139
University Church 19
Upper Mount Street xxxii
Usher's Island 65, 68
Usher's Quay 65

Victoria Quay 65, 68
Viking Adventure Centre 44

Vikings vii, 44, 45, 46, 78, 87, 132, 135, 150

Wellington Monument 70
Wexford 159–60
Whitefriar Street Church 119
Wicklow xiii, *142*, 144–5, 150–51
Wicklow Gap 156
Wicklow Street 24

Wilde, Oscar 9, 32
Wine bar xviii
Winetavern Street 46
Wood Quay 63
Writers' Museum, *see under* Dublin

Yeats, W.B. 20, 31, 106, 107

Zoo 70–71